The Pioneer Village Cookbook

Reliable Receipts
&
Curious Remedies

by
Ann Chandonnet

"I strongly suspect that some of the Pilgrim Fathers must have come over to this country with the Cookery book under one arm and the Bible under the other."
--an English visitor to America, 1836

Native Ground Books & Music
Order Number: NGB-960   ISBN 978-1-883206-60-4
Library of Congress Control Number 2010923696
© 2010 Native Ground Books & Music

CONTENTS

O PIONEER

Growing up on an apple and dairy farm, I came to appreciate the simplicity of America's pioneer roots. Our extended household included my grandmother, who was born in 1888. "Gram" gardened, canned, cooked, and sewed with methods that today seem like marvelous secrets. Some of my early delights were sitting at her knee, helping to wind balls of yarn for mittens, or watching as she rolled out pie crust. Her skill at making something from nothing, combined with the pleasures of browsing her 19th-century cookbooks, fed my desire to collect old recipes or "receipts" of earlier times.

This book is an invitation to join me as we lift the latch and walk into the kitchens of our pioneer ancestors. Using many authentic recipes, we'll recreate the meals that were cooked over open campfires and in bubbling pots in the hearth. For this book, we'll define pioneer cooking as any dish Daniel Boone would have eaten with relish.

As a boy in Birdsboro, Pennsylvania, in the mid 1730s, Boone breakfasted on bread, milk and pie; dined at noon on pork and a wheat flour pudding and consumed milk and cornmeal mush in the evening. Even as a child, Boone contributed food to the table, bagging small game with a club. By the age of 12, he had his own rifle.

Pioneer housewives like Boone's mother purchased salt, molasses and flour but little else. For holidays, the larder might boast raisins, sugar, or perhaps a costly nutmeg or lemon. Fancy food was rare, but Daniel's wife Rebecca could whip up a mean Indian Pudding.

Hart's Square Village

3

O PIONEER

With game plentiful, pioneers regularly dined on such delicacies as hare, squirrel, wild fowl, turkey, bear, raccoon and deer. Wild greens, roots and berries supplemented garden crops. Pigs were not native to North America until Spanish explorer Hernando de Soto introduced Iberian swine to Florida in 1539. With plenty of acorns for forage, the pigs multiplied, and pioneers happily erected smoke houses to preserve hams and sidemeat.

Life was hard for the first settlers. Faced with dense forests with little cleared land, pioneers thinned these endless woods by girdling trees with an axe. With the ground open to sunlight, survival crops were planted among the stumps. Within a few years, the neatly cleared plots were sown with corn, wheat, oats and rye. Potatoes, beans and peas were planted nearby, with beds of savory and medicinal herbs at the kitchen door. Orchards were set out, and over time provided ample supplies of juicy apples, pears, peaches and plums.

If you have a taste for pioneer life, it's not too late. Take heart in the fact that you can tread the paths of pioneer villages from the Atlantic to the Pacific. (Some are listed on pp. 153-159). In these settlements of restored or reconstructed log buildings, expert interpreters answer questions, cultivate boneset and thyme, plow with oxen, herd Devon cattle and simmer stews. Often clad in pioneer garb, the interpreters demonstrate skills like shoeing horses, peeling logs, shearing sheep and weaving coverlets. Many of the following recipes came from the collections of these villages.

So venture forth, resourceful Pioneer, knife and spoon in hand! Tie on an apron. Join the fun.

PIONEER ROOTS

Log construction was first introduced to the New World by Swedes and Finns who settled Delaware in the 1640s. The Scotch-Irish carried log construction south from Pennsylvania along the Great Wagon Road. The two basic log styles are round and hewn. Round logs are simply peeled, while hewn logs are squared off on all four sides with an adz or broad axe. Where the logs meet, there are several different styles, such as V-notch and half-dovetail. Spaces between the logs were chinked with a mixture of clay and straw. A well-chinked cabin was insulated from a harsh winter. Windows were few, which helped to conserve heat in the winter. Many of these cabins measure only 10x12 or 14x16 feet. Touring them today, it's hard to imagine a family of 11 bedding down. Pallets must have crowded both the loft and the main floor.

Examples of log cabin construction can be seen at pioneer villages up and down this land. If a cabin has not been restored to its original appearance, it may be difficult to recognize. That's because as soon as sawmills were built, a pioneer's wife often insisted that siding should be added to the outside of their cabin. Besides transforming their rustic hut into a fine house, siding added needed insulation to the dwelling.

PIONEER ROOTS

At Kings Mountain State Park History Farm, for example, the blacksmith/carpenter shop (c. 1820) was discovered to be a log structure within the walls of a frame house being demolished in Kershaw County, North Carolina. As pioneer families grew, tiny one-room cabins were often enlarged by enclosing a porch or connecting the original cabin to a second cabin with an open breezeway, called a "dog trot."

Isolated pioneer families made an annual trek to a general store to buy provisions. The General Store at Walnut Grove Pioneer Village reproduces these provisions in its bins and barrels. Barrels hold lard, coffee, peanuts, all purpose flour, sugar, crackers and cookies. Bins hold macaroni, rice and whole wheat flour. The kids in the family usually headed for the glass jars holding peppermint sticks, licorice pipes or horehound drops — and then held their breaths. At the O.D. Murray & Co. general store in Catawba County, North Carolina, kids were tempted by wooden toys and

rock candy, while their parents dickered for cornmeal and oatmeal (fresh from Murray's Mill), overalls, yard goods and felt hats.

PIONEER ROOTS

At Jamestown in 1607, settlers ate salted fish brought from Britain and tried new foods they learned about from the Powhatan Indians. Among the latter dishes were corn dumplings and hearty stews of corn, squash, and beans. The newcomers delighted in venison and fresh  fish. Most of the time they dined on puddings, pies, pottage (a stew with very little meat) or gruel made of oatmeal, raisins and milk. Some Jamestown repasts were based on receipts published by Elinore Fettiplace in 1604.

During their first winter, Jamestown's settlers ate anything they could catch or gather—including sturgeon, turtle, gulls, snakes, raccoons and oysters. By the fall of 1608, John Smith wrote, "The rivers became so covered with swans, geese, ducks, and cranes that we daily feasted with good bread, Virginia peas, pumpions, and putshamins [persimmons], fish, fowl, and diverse sorts of wild beasts as fat as we could eat them."

JAMESTOWN POTTAGE
--Jamestown-Yorktown Foundation

2 tablespoons fresh breadcrumbs	**a pinch of saffron**
1 egg yolk	**1 cup milk**
1 teaspoon chopped parsley	**1½ cup cooked fresh peas**
½ teaspoon ground ginger	

Beat together bread crumbs, egg yolk, parsley, salt, ginger and saffron. Bring the milk almost to a boil. Pour in peas and bread crumb mixture. Bring to a boil, stirring constantly. Serve at once. Yield: 3 servings.

PIONEER ROOTS

America's European settlers came from all over the Continent, and their origins affected what they ate. Pioneers of German origin favored pork and cabbage, hot potato salad, Sauerbraten (pot roast seasoned with crumbs of gingersnaps or rye bread), cabbage in yeast pastry and sauerkraut. Venison turned up in German stew (Hirschbrust) as well as Swedish potato sausage and Italian pork sausage. Dutch communities downed pigs-in-blankets. The Pennsylvania Dutch snacked on soft pretzels. Scandinavians sat down to "white meals" composed entirely of dairy products.

As coastal areas became occupied, the descendants of the first settlers pushed further west, exploring new rivers, finding fertile valleys with good supplies of water. They encountered foods like wild rice, maple syrup, persimmons, hickory nuts, possum and catfish. The proverbial "melting pot" embraced all sorts of Old World traditions and New World comestibles.

SNOW CABBAGE
--from *Country Cooking* (1907)

Chop very fine a medium-sized head of cabbage. Beat together 1 cup rich sour cream, 2 tablespoonfuls good cider vinegar, 1 large tablespoonful sugar, salt and pepper to suit the taste. Whip until white and creamy; pour over cabbage. Serve at once. Yield: 6 servings.

PIONEER ROOTS

Fritters were considered a way to gild leftovers—everything from mashed parsnips to corn kernels and apples.

PALATABLE FRITTERS
        --Mrs. J. F. Byers, Tokio, Oklahoma, 1907

Take 1 egg, 1 cup of milk, ½ teaspoonfuls of salt, 1 of baking powder, and 1 of sugar. Add flour to make a thick batter; then add 1 cup of leftover meat, fruit or vegetables chopped fine, and fry in frying pan   full of hot grease. This is a good dish for supper or breakfast.

If pioneers lived at great distances from fairs, stores and roads, self-sufficiency was their way of life. Should they live near a town, fish and fruit might be available by the barrel.

For example, in a letter written from Raleigh on January 19, 1849, North Carolina legislator John Y. Hicks describes the crops of Macon County: Indian corn, oats, wheat, rye, hay, Irish and sweet potatoes, cabbage, buckwheat and fruits such as apples. Domestic animals included hogs, cattle, and sheep.

A letter written that same month by legislator/merchant/farmer Kader Biggs cites fisheries on Albermarle Sound where shad, herring, rock and bass flourished.

Photo by Wayne Erbsen

He saw a haul made in 1845 or '46 of 18,000 rock or bass, averaging 40 pounds each. "The beach was 50 yards wide and 150 yards long and one could walk on fish from one side to the other," Biggs wrote.

THE THREE SISTERS

From friendly Native American neighbors, settlers learned about the three sisters: corn, beans and squash. These nutritious vegetables, native to the Americas, were important foods. Indians consumed them in countless combinations, most often in a stew combining beans with corn and fish or game. The Narragansett called this dish *msickquatash*. I grew up in Massachusetts eating succotash prepared with shell beans, similar to cranberry beans. The Pennsylvania Dutch prepare succotash with milk or cream. The Mohegan version included bear grease. This is the 1907 Kansas variation:

SUCCOTASH

> 2 quarts fresh string beans
> 1 quart green corn cut from cob
> salt, pepper and butter size of an egg (3 tablespoons)
> 1 cup milk
> 2 tablespoons cornstarch

Prepare string beans, cut into pieces, and cook in water to cover until crisp-tender. Add corn. Cook 4 minutes. Add salt, pepper and butter. Just before serving, mix milk with cornstarch. Stir into pot until liquid is thickened.
Yield: 10 servings.

The Cherokee favored a kind of bean bread, cooked as dumplings. In the Appalachians, Native Americans harvested the American Lotus (a water lily) from ponds. Its young leaves were cooked like spinach. Its tubers were baked, and the ripe seeds were ground into flour or simmered into porridge. Ramps were one of the first edible plants gathered in spring. Their leaves and bulbs were sliced and added to stews. In the fall, butternuts were gathered, the meats ground to a paste with a mortar and pestle, and this "butter" was spread on corn cakes or steamed chestnut bread.

THE THREE SISTERS

Farmsteads in the South often grew sorghum cane to produce their own sweetener. When the cane was harvested, it was squeezed through the rollers of a mill. The juice collected was boiled until enough water evaporated to leave a thick, dark syrup. The "cooker" often took the form of a waist-high outdoor hearth under a roof that protected the evaporating juice from rain. This was the Southern equivalent of the maple syrup harvest in New England. Sorghum looks something like molasses, but has its own delicious flavor.

DEERFIELD SQUASH
 --Pioneer Valley Growers, South Deerfield, MA

   1 butternut squash, peeled, seeded and cut in chunks
   1 quart water
   butter, brown sugar, honey, sorghum and/or maple
      syrup to taste.

Bring the water to a boil. Add the prepared squash. Cover. Cook until tender. Drain well. Mash and season to taste with remaining ingredients plus salt and pepper. Yield: depends on size of squash.

THE THREE SISTERS

PURSLANE SALAD

Purslane has glossy plump leaves and a lemony flavor. This nutritious wild green is sometimes available at farmers' markets.

> 3 tablespoons oil
> 1 tablespoon lemon juice
> 2 tablespoons finely chopped onion
> 1 cup halved cherry tomatoes or chopped tomatoes
> 6 cups purslane sprigs and leaves
> 4 cups flat-leaf parsley leaves
> edible flowers for garnish

Whisk together oil, lemon juice, onion and salt and pepper to taste in a large bowl. Add remaining ingredients and toss gently to coat. Garnish with edible chive flowers or pansy blossoms. (Choose flowers that have not been sprayed with insecticide.) Serve salad at once with hot biscuits and ham.

Yield: 6 servings.

Early Kentucky pioneers were considered "settled" when they had cleared enough land to raise corn. The corncrib adjoining the Hunsucker Cabin at Hart's Square emphasizes the role of corn in the North Carolina pioneer diet. At the Noah "Bud" Ogle saddlebag cabin, now a part of Great Smoky Mountains National Park, corn and apples were the main crops. At the 1817 grist mill in Spring Mill State Park (near Mitchell, Indiana), visitors can watch corn being ground into meal. Texas pioneers ate corn at almost every meal, everything from hull corn to cornmeal mush to cornbread with crabapple jelly.

> *In planting corn, four kernels to a hill: one for the blackbird, one for the crow, one for the cutworm, and one to grow.*

THE PIONEER HEARTH

Harold Warp Pioneer Village features kitchens demonstrating a hundred years of change in Nebraska cooking methods: a fireplace (1830), a wood-burning Franklin stove (1860), an iron cook stove with an oven (1890) and a stove fueled by natural gas (1930). The Harold Warp museum has preserved receipts for dyes and medicines.

The pioneer hearth served three purposes: heating, drying and cooking. Damp clothes, clouts (rags used as towels or diapers), herbs, bean pods, and slices of apple, pumpkin or squash could be hung there to dry. Hearths were large, often taking up most of an end wall. The 1825 Hawkins House in Waynesville, Ohio, boasts a central chimney, heating two rooms. The chimney measures eight feet square at its base, with two six foot by five and a half foot fire places, back-to-back.

The best chimneys were field stone, cut stone or firebrick. They were made massive in order to retain all possible heat and withstand wind storms. Some were equipped with fire backs, metal plates that reflected heat outward to the room.

Iron andirons or "fire dogs" stood within the hearth to support logs, so drafts could encourage the flames from beneath.

Pots stood on legs on the floor of the hearth. A "spider" was a cast iron pot with three legs. Skillets with long handles sometimes perched on separate stands with three legs, to ease the weary arms of the housewife. Demonstrations of hearth cooking delight visitors to the Wheelwright House at Strawbery Banke and in the kitchens of Colonial Williamsburg.

Treated correctly, cast iron kitchenware lasts. A 9-inch skillet in the collection of the Pioneer-Krier Museum in Ashland, Kansas, was used by the Bare family from 1889 to 1960.

THE PIONEER HEARTH

If cast iron pots are rusty or sticky, season them.

SEASONING CAST IRON
Clean the pan well. Use steel wool if it is old and rusty. Smear all over with solid shortening such as Crisco. Bake on a cookie sheet lined with parchment at 200° for 2 hours.

Pioneer cooking became a little easier with the invention of the trammel hook—a device with links or openings at different heights for hanging a pothook in the fireplace. A fireplace usually had two trammels—one for the large tea kettle and one for the stew pot. Water would be heating in the tea kettle at all times.

The family stew was often a continuous affair to which beans, greens, grains, herbs, roots and meat were added when available. This time-honored *pot-au-feu* (from the French "pot on the fire") was simply meat or bones boiled with beans or grains and vegetables. Typically, a ladle dipped out the solids as the first course, while the savory broth was served separately as a second course, over or with bread. From this custom, we get the phrase "take pot luck." It could be lima beans and ham hocks on Monday, limas and potatoes Tuesday, limas and parsnips with wild garlic and onions Wednesday, and so on. The rhyme about "pease porridge nine days old" takes on new meaning when one understands this way of life. Meals were commonly monotonous, sometimes lacking even salt.

Pioneers worked so hard from sunup to sundown that any food was good food. Creamed blackbird on sippets (toast fingers) was welcome.

> *If housekeeper can have but one kind of pan, it will be wise to have the cast-iron kind.*
> --Maria Parloa, 1887

THE PIONEER HEARTH

Photo by Wayne Erbsen

OLD PEASE SOUP

Put a pound and a half of split peas on in four quarts of water, with roast-beef or mutton bones, and a ham bone, two heads of celery, and four onions, let them boil till the peas are sufficiently soft to pulp through a sieve, strain it, put it into the pot with pepper and salt, and boil it nearly one hour. Two or three handfuls of spinach, well washed and cut a little, added when the soup is strained, is a great improvement....

--Sara Josepha Hale, *The Good Housekeeper* (1841)

O de times is very hard
I'm goin' get me a dime's worth o' lard
I'm goin' keep my skillet greasy if I can.
If I can, can, can, if I can, can, can,
I'm goin' keep my skillet greasy if I can.
--A folk song

LITTLE HOUSE ON THE PRAIRIE

Wash on Monday
Iron on Tuesday
Mend on Wednesday
Churn on Thursday
Clean on Friday
Bake on Saturday
Rest on Sunday

Photo by Wayne Erbsen

Delicious food is a keystone of the nine "Little House" books by Laura Ingalls Wilder. Ma had a cookstove in Wisconsin, but cooked on an open hearth when the family moved to Kansas. In 1876, when they moved to the banks of Plum Creek, Ma had a new iron cookstove with a real oven.

Pa hunted and farmed. Ma prepared and preserved. They grew grain, and then Pa ground it in the coffee grinder as Ma prepared to bake bread. The family ate ripe tomatoes with cream and sugar. Raw turnip was a winter snack. Pumpkin was stewed slowly all day until the water boiled away, and the vegetable turned rich and brown. Sunday dinner featured Rye n' Injun bread, chicken pie made from hens "too old to lay," gravy, baked beans, salt pork and pickled beets.

From the warmth of Wilder's prose, filled with spice and everything nice, the reader understands how good food helped pioneers weather the discomforts of frontier life.

LITTLE HOUSE ON THE PRAIRIE

PICKLED BEETS

Cooks who garden often can these for winter. If you harvest 35 pounds of beets, you can count on about 36 pints of canned pickled beets in the larder. The "pickle" (liquid) left when a jar of beets is opened is sometimes recycled to pickle hardboiled eggs.

Photo by Wayne Erbsen

12 to 16 small beets
½ cup sugar
1¼ cups vinegar
½ teaspoon salt
1 tablespoon whole
pickling spices

Wash beets well. Cut off tops about an inch above roots. Cook in boiling water until tender, 30 to 40 minutes. Cool. Slip off skins, and trim tops. Slice or leave whole.

Combine sugar, vinegar and salt in saucepan. Tie spices in small square of cheesecloth or enclose in a tea ball. Add to vinegar. Simmer mixture 15 minutes. Add beets. Bring to boiling. Remove from heat. Discard spices. Cool. Chill before serving. Yield: 6 servings.

LITTLE HOUSE ON THE PRAIRIE

For the Ingalls family, hog butchering time meant holding the pig's skinned tail in front of the cookstove grate until it browned and sizzled.

Parched corn was a dish often on the Thanksgiving table.

PARCHED CORN

First dry your corn. Peel shucks from corn on the cob, but do not rip them away from the stem. Tie string tightly around the shucks, and hang up the ears to dry in a warm place for several days. Then cut the kernels off the cobs. You need 3 to 4 ears of corn to make 2 cups of kernels.

> **2 cups dried corn kernels**
> **2 tablespoons lard or bacon drippings**
> **salt**

Melt the lard in a skillet. The fat will be hot enough when one kernel sizzles. Add corn and stir until all the kernels are puffed and dark brown. (A few may pop). Drain on paper towels. Salt. Serve warm. This is a traditional Native American snack food.

Yield: 4 servings.

One Ingalls' Christmas table featured both a suckling pig with an apple in its mouth and a fat roast goose.

During the summer in Wisconsin's Big Woods, Ma made her own hard cheese. When blackbirds invaded the corn crop, she baked blackbird pie. Picked by the bushel, seedy-but-flavorful huckleberries were turned into jelly, jam, pie and pudding.

Beverages Ma prepared included eggnog, ginger water (Switchell), cambric tea (hot water and milk with very little tea), and lemonade. Coffee was most often sweetened with brown sugar or molasses.

LITTLE HOUSE ON THE PRAIRIE

SWITCHELL

Switchell was a refreshing summer drink, usually concocted during haymaking. The housewife would carry pitchers of the mixture to the hayfield. Its unusual name may be related to "swizzle" — a stick or rod used for stirring mixed drinks. The term originated in the United States about 1800, and was first used in print in Parson Weems' famous biography of George Washington. Weems described it as a Yankee drink.

> **2 quarts hot water**
> **1 cup sugar**
> **½ cup molasses**
> **½ cup vinegar**
> **½ teaspoon ground ginger**

Mix all ingredients, being sure that the molasses is well dissolved. Allow to cool. Serve cold. Yield: 9 cups.

Quisenburg Ranch, Cherry County, Nebraska

WAGONS HO!

Long before the Chisholm Trail or the Oregon Trail, heavily laden wagons carved ruts along the Wilderness Road. This route was traveled by 300,000 pioneers who followed Daniel Boone through the Cumberland Gap.

Those hardy pioneers hunted and consumed Eastern elk as well as woodland buffalo—grazers from the wandering herds of Eastern bison that roamed far from the Great Plains. Bison lie behind place names like North Carolina's "Meat Camp." The last Eastern woodland bison was killed at Valley Head, West Virginia, in 1825.

Despite its leanness, buffalo has a rich flavor, does not shrink when cooked, and is about 30 percent higher in protein than beef. It is lower in cholesterol and calories than beef, lamb, chicken, turkey, salmon and even tuna.

GREAT HUMPED BACK ROAST
    --National Buffalo Association, Fort St. Pierre, S.D.

    3 to 5 lbs. inexpensive cut buffalo meat
    1 cup vinegar
    2 cups strong black coffee
    salt and pepper
    garlic or onion
    cooking oil
    2 cups water

One or two days before: With a large knife, cut slits completely through the meat. Insert slivers of garlic and/or onion. Pour vinegar over meat. Cover and refrigerate for 24 to 48 hours.

When ready to cook: Heat oil in a heavy pot—cast iron if possible. Brown roast until nearly burned on all sides. Pour coffee over meat. Add water and cover. Simmer on top of stove or in 325° oven for 4 to 6 hours. Season with salt and pepper 20 minutes before serving. The resulting black gravy may be thickened or served as is.

WAGONS HO!

Pioneers followed many well-traveled trails such as the Natchez Trace, the Mormon, the Oregon and the California trails. Zane's Trace, used from 1797 to about 1820, ran from Pittsburgh, Pennsylvania, to Maysville, Kentucky.

Emigrants to the California gold rush, to Pike's Peak or along the Oregon Trail carried food supplies in their wagons, supplementing that grub with game shot and fish caught along the way. *The Emigrants' Guide to Oregon and California* (1845) gave these recommendations: "In procuring supplies for this journey, the emigrant should provide himself with, at least, 200 pounds of flour, 150 pounds of bacon; ten pounds of coffee; twenty pounds of sugar; and ten pounds of salt."

An article published March 19, 1847, in the St. Joseph, Missouri, *Gazette* added rice, beans, dried fruit, saleratus, soap, cheese, dried pumpkin, onions and cornmeal.

On June 11, 1838, along the Oregon Trail, Sarah Smith penned these words: "Have just taken our supper of buffalo. We love it very much when it is cooked good as it was to-night. Mr. Gray and Mr. Smith are cooks. They sometimes boil & fry, sometimes chop it and make it appear like sausage. After it is fried, make a milk gravy & it is very fine."

SARAH SMITH'S BUFFALO GRAVY
--Whitman Mission National Historic Site

> **1 pound ground bison or beef**
> **4 tablespoons flour**
> **salt and pepper**
> **2 cups milk**

In a heavy skillet or Dutch oven, brown meat, breaking it apart into chunks as it cooks. Cook until it loses its red color. Salt and pepper to taste. Stir in flour. Stir constantly while adding milk. Cook until thickened. Serve hot. Yield: 4 servings.

WAGONS HO!

Today's cooks make a distinction between game and meat; the pioneers observed no such differentiation. *American Cookery* (1796) includes recipes for rabbit, goose, woodcock, snipe, partridge and pigeon as well as turtle. Scots-Irish pioneers curried rabbit, and put almost any red meat into a Mince — finely chopped or ground meat scrambled with diced onion and served with boiled potatoes. Basic British recipes were cut to fit the local cloth; Mark Twain, for instance, expressed his delight in prairie chicken made into pot pie.

RABBIT SAUTĚ

Dried mushrooms may be added to taste.
¼ teaspoon freshly ground black pepper
½ teaspoon dried thyme
½ teaspoon dried oregano
2 tablespoons flour
1 rabbit (about 2 pounds), cut into serving pieces
2 tablespoons oil
2 cloves garlic, minced
3 bay leaves
8 small boiling onions, peeled
1½ cups chicken stock

In a plate, combine black pepper, thyme, oregano and flour. Dredge rabbit in the mixture. In a large skillet, soup pot or Dutch oven, heat oil. Add rabbit and sauté over medium heat until just brown, about 7 minutes.

Add garlic, bay leaves, onions and stock and bring to a boil. Immediately reduce heat to medium-low. Cover loosely and simmer on the stove top or in the hearth until rabbit has cooked through, about half an hour. Remove bay leaves before serving. Serve hot with cornbread and greens, squash, pumpkin or broccoli. Yield: 4 servings.

WAGONS HO!

MOLASSES PUDDING
--National Historic Oregon Trail Interpretive Center

> ½ cup molasses
> ½ cup milk
> 2 cups flour
> ½ cup melted butter or lard
> 1 teaspoon baking soda
> ½ teaspoon salt
> 1 cup seeded raisins (optional)

Combine molasses and milk. Add in butter, baking soda and salt. Add flour, half a cup at a time. Add raisins. Pour dough into a buttered bread pan. Put pan on top of pebbles in a large kettle of slow-boiling, shallow water. Water should come up halfway on bread pan. Cover and steam 1¼ hours. Serve sliced.

These biscuits are baked in a sheet — eliminating the need for a rolling pin, a floured surface and a biscuit cutter.

TEA BISCUITS
--Whitman Mission National Historic Site

> 1 cup butter
> 1 cup milk
> 4 eggs
> 3 cups all-purpose flour
> 1 teaspoon salt
> 1½ teaspoons baking soda
> 2 teaspoons cream of tartar

Cream butter. Beat in eggs. Then beat in milk. Mix in remaining ingredients. Spread evenly in a 9x13-inch greased and floured pan. Bake at 350° or 20 to 30 minutes or until it tests done. Break into chunks. Serve warm with butter and honey.

WAGONS HO!

Born in upstate New York, pioneer Narcissa Whitman was one of the first white women to cross the continent overland. She and her husband Marcus founded a mission among the Cayuse Indians of Oregon. In a letter dated August 11, 1836, she wrote about frying unleavened biscuits to serve with fresh salmon. This is a modernized version of her recipe.

NARCISSA'S CAMP BREAD
--Whitman Mission National Historic Site

1 cup flour
½ cup water
1½ teaspoons baking powder
½ teaspoon salt
fat for frying (beef tallow, shortening, bacon fat, etc.)

Mix water, flour, baking powder and salt together. Stir and knead to form a smooth dough. Turn onto a lightly floured board and form into a rough square about half an inch thick. Cut into 2-inch squares.

Melt fat in a heavy skillet or Dutch oven. When a drop of water sizzles in the fat, place dough squares on bottom in a single layer. Cook at medium heat until lightly browned. Turn over and cook other side. Serve hot.

MEALS WITHOUT "RECEIPTS"

Peasants and pioneers were usually bookless except for the family Bible. As a result, recipes were passed down from person to person, learned at the cook's elbow. Some medieval recipes were put into rhyme in order to make memorizing them easier. British poet John Gay sent this recipe to a clergyman friend:

A KNUCKLE OF VEAL
Take a knuckle of veal,
You may buy it or steal,
In a few pieces cut it,
In a stewing-pan put it;
Salt, pepper, mace
Must season this knuckle.
-- *All the Year Round* (1868)

Gay continues at some length. He adds sorrel, celery, thyme, spinach, endive, lettuce, beets and pot marigold to his knuckle and simmers it with the cover on "Thrice as long as you preach." That could indicate six to nine hours of simmering!

It's amusing to browse in old cookbooks, but use good sense if you attempt the receipts. In Pierre Blot's 1863 cookbook, for example, he recommends stuffing opossum, otter, raccoon, skunk, woodchuck or fox with leaves of sage, bay, mint and thyme. That sounds reasonable, but Blot follows with: "and sew it up. Hang it outside in a place sheltered from the sun, such as the northern side of a building; leave it thus five or six days, then take off and cook." It's likely meat hung for such a long period would be slightly ripe — perhaps harmful to eat.

MEALS WITHOUT "RECEIPTS"

ONE assumes the following dressing is intended for coleslaw or, as some early cookbooks have it, "cold slaw."

VERY NICE DRESSING FOR CABBAGE
--manuscript cookbook of Mrs. S. W. Johnson, begun in 1867 in New Hampshire

1 egg
4 tablespoons cream or milk
6 tablespoons vinegar
a piece of butter the size of a walnut
**   [2 tablespoons]**
a little pepper & salt
a tablespoon of mustard

Beat them well together. Put it on the fire and stir till it thickens. When cold, pour it over the cabbage, chopped fine.

MEALS WITHOUT "RECEIPTS"

A few "receipts" were coded with Bible verses as a way to combine lessons in religion with instruction in cooking. Probably both the Bible and the receipt became smeared with flour and butter as the directions were laboriously deciphered.

SCRIPTURE CAKE

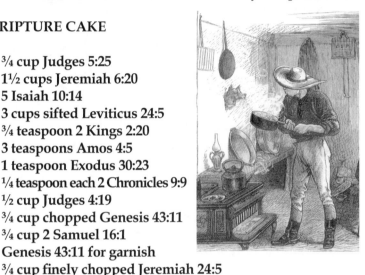

¾ cup Judges 5:25
1½ cups Jeremiah 6:20
5 Isaiah 10:14
3 cups sifted Leviticus 24:5
¾ teaspoon 2 Kings 2:20
3 teaspoons Amos 4:5
1 teaspoon Exodus 30:23
¼ teaspoon each 2 Chronicles 9:9
½ cup Judges 4:19
¾ cup chopped Genesis 43:11
¾ cup 2 Samuel 16:1
Genesis 43:11 for garnish
¾ cup finely chopped Jeremiah 24:5

Cream butter and sugar until light and fluffy. Beat in egg yolks, one at a time, mixing well after each addition. Sift together flour, salt, baking powder, cinnamon, nutmeg, ginger and powdered allspice.

Beat flour mixture into butter mixture, alternating with milk, until flour is just blended.

Beat room-temperature egg whites until stiff; fold into batter. Fold in chopped nuts, figs and raisins. Grease and flour a 10 inch tube pan. Put in batter. Bake at 325° until a cake tester comes out clean, 50 to 70 minutes. Cool on a wire rack for 15 minutes. Then turn cake out of pan. When cool, drizzle with Burnt Jeremiah Syrup. Garnish with whole almonds.

MEALS WITHOUT "RECEIPTS"

BURNT JEREMIAH SYRUP

1½ cups Jeremiah 6:20
½ cup Genesis 24:45
¼ cup Genesis

In a saucepan over low heat, melt sugar, stirring occasionally to prevent sticking. When sugar is melted, continue stirring and cooking until it is a deep golden color. Add water and cook, stirring, until smooth. Remove from heat, stir in butter. Cool. Drizzle over cooled cake.

Itinerant preachers, who served their most distant parishioners on horseback, were usually served the best dinner the housewife could put together, often beginning with fried chicken. Scripture Cake would have made an ideal finish to the meal on such occasions.

Photo by Wayne Erbsen

MEALS WITHOUT "RECEIPTS"

The first European cookbooks were written by professional chefs for consultation by other professionals.

Pioneer and colonial cooks who could write often compiled their own manuscript manuals. One of the best examples is the small, handwritten volume bound in brown leather that Martha Washington's family brought from England to America. Mrs. Washington consulted it while she was First Lady (1789-97). The book contained more than 500 recipes. Martha handed it down to her granddaughter, Eleanor Parke Custis, on the occasion of Eleanor's wedding.

Engaged young women would copy from their mother's handbooks, which usually contained, in addition to recipes, directions on how to remove stains, occupy young children, set a table, arrange food artfully, use ingredients thriftfully, deal with leftovers, prepare remedies and preserve food.

One published cookbook available to pioneers was Hannah Glasse's *The Art of Cookery Made Plain and Easy*, printed in London in 1742, 1747 and 1796. Stocked at a china shop, it proved very popular with both colonials and Britons. Virginia editions came off presses in Alexandria in 1805 and 1812.

Another British book, Mrs. Mary Cole's *The Lady's Complete Guide; or Cookery in All its Branches* (1788), criticizes Hannah Glasse for plagiarizing most of her recipes. However, Mrs. Cole credited some of her recipes to eminent French cooks — persons who seem to have been figments of her imagination.

MEALS WITHOUT "RECEIPTS"

The first wholly American cookbook was *American Cookery* by Amelia Simmons, published in 1796 in Hartford, Connecticut. It was just 47 pages, and sold out quickly. Simmons was the first to document New World ingredients like squash and Jerusalem artichokes and record recipes like Pumpkin Pie, Cramberry Sauce, Johnny Cakes, Spruce Beer and Indian Pudding. Simmons, who cooked on an open hearth, provided recipes for five different gingerbreads — chiefly the hard cookie that traveled well with infantry men and school children. She added butter, rose water, brandy, nutmeg, eggs and coriander with a lavish hand. To follow her sketchy recipes, the cook had to know what she was doing.

SIMMONS' POMPKIN PIE
One quart of milk, 1 pint pompkin, 4 eggs, molasses, allspice and ginger in a crust, bake 1 hour.

A STEW PIE
-- Amelia Simmons
Boil a shoulder of Veal, and cut up, salt, pepper, and butter half pound, and slices of raw salt pork, make a layer of meat, and a layer of biscuit, or biscuit dough into a pot, cover close and stew half an hour in three quarts of water only.

MEALS WITHOUT "RECEIPTS"

Following in Simmons' footsteps was Eliza Leslie, whose *Directions for Cookery* ran to 60 editions between 1837 and 1870. Leslie includes an Oyster Pie recipe in which puff paste crusts are baked blind (empty), and the hot oysters and gravy are inserted just before the dish goes to table.

As the nineteenth century drew to a close, recipes became more and more specific, and soon included lists of ingredients with precise quantities and careful directions. Out went "butter size of an egg" and in came measuring cups and spoons.

At Walnut Grove Pioneer Village in Iowa, volunteer Ronita Farren demonstrates pioneer cooking in the summer kitchen wearing an outfit she sewed herself. She cooks without written recipes: "The recipes I cook are recipes that my Grandmother taught me when I was a little girl. They are part of my family's oral tradition. My Grandmother never wrote down a recipe and that is how she taught them to me. 'She showed them and told them,' is how I put it."

An apple tree puts to shame all the men and women that have attempted to dress since the world began.
--Henry Ward Beecher (1862)

MEALS WITHOUT "RECEIPTS"

"One of the more interesting things that I have experienced when I am demonstrating in the summer kitchen is when I make egg noodles from scratch," says Farren. "I roll them out and let them dry. Then I generally make homemade chicken or beef noodle soup. People are really fascinated by the process of making noodles. It always helps me drive home the point that in pioneer days you had to make everything by hand. You could not just go to the store and buy a box of noodles. I don't think people really stop and think about that. At least not until you see someone having to make noodles," Farren said.

Farren does all her cooking on an antique cast iron stove. "I explain to visitors that most pioneer woman did not have such a nice stove or complete summer kitchen to cook in. Many women only had a open fire and maybe a tree or lean-to for shade."

These are some of the dishes Farren prepares: Chicken or Beef Noodle Soup, Beans and Corn Bread, White and Wheat Bread, Peach Cobbler, Green Beans and Bacon.

USING OLD "RECEIPTS"

Today's cooks harbor a growing interest in our edible roots. Inspired by selecting produce at a farmers' market, they seek out vegetables beyond French fries. They grow herbs. They sign up for classes in butchering, sausage-making or elaborate pastry. They learn to recognize edible wild mushrooms and dry them for stews and sauces.

Because readers may want to try some of the recipes herein, most of them appear in modern form with precise measurements and temperatures. Just for fun, however, I've included period recipes like this:

TO MAKE CHERRY TARTS

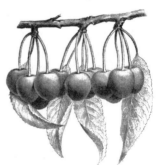

Stone your Cherries, lay them in the Tarts, with abundance of Sugar and Cinnamon, Cordecidron and Orange Peill, close up the Tarts, and send them to the Oven.

--Mrs. McLintock's Receipts for Cookery and Pastry Work, 1736.

As evidenced by this tart recipe, Scotland's first cookbook, *Mrs. McLintock's Receipts*, expects the cook to know a great deal concerning pastry, sweetening and oven temperature. McLintock also expects the reader to deal with entire hindquarters of lamb and haunches of venison. To make a Seed Cake, one must be physically capable of beating three dozen eggs with 3 pounds of sugar "until thick and white." Time is not of the essence; a recipe for Candied Angelica takes 10 days. Furthermore, McLintock's recipes call for a "mutchkin" of barm, a "blade" of mace and a "gill" of brandy. Use the definitions on the following pages to interpret pioneer recipes.

> *Never praise your Cider, Horse, or Bedfellow.*
> --Benjamin Franklin, 1736

PIONEER COOKING TERMS

Barm: a form of yeast.

Blade: a leaf; a segment of the outer layer of a nutmeg shell.

Brawn: a molded, jellied meat dish, usually made from a pig's head, but also prepared with sheep, wild boar, ox or moose. Also called head cheese.

Butter the size of an egg: about a quarter cup.

Callops: bacon or thin slices of ham.

Clabber: sour milk.

Cordecidron: lemon peel.

Drop: 1/16 ounce.

Dutch oven or "bake-kettle": A large cast iron pot for hearth cooking, with a rimmed cover to hold coals.

Emptins: a form of yeast made from the dregs of beer.

Ferment: a sourdough yeast made from apples or pumpkins.

Filé: a powder of sassafras leaves; used as a thickening and seasoning agent in gumbo.

Fish eyes: large tapioca beads.

Flitch: unsmoked slab bacon.

Forcemeat: stuffing for anything from venison to cabbage. This could be a simple bread dressing or include bacon, lemon juice, chopped veal, mushrooms, truffles, cayenne, herbs, etc.

Funeral or burial biscuits: Hard cookies flavored with caraway seeds and stamped with wooden relief molds featuring a rose, a heart, etc.

Gammon: either slab bacon or ham hocks.

Gem pan: muffin pan, patented by Nathanial Waterman of Boston in 1859.

Gill: half a cup or four fluid ounces.

Graham flour: Whole wheat or "unbolted" flour, named for Sylvester Graham.

Hirschhornsalz or harts horn: a refined salt made from the ash of deer antlers, used as baking powder.

Indian or Injun meal: cornmeal.

Lib: a pound plus one ounce and 8 drams.

PIONEER COOKING TERMS

Photo by Wayne Erbsen

Mutchkin: slightly less than a pint.

Pandowdy: a dessert of fruit topped with biscuit and baked; cousin to the cobbler, grunt and slump. During baking, the crust is broken up and pressed down ("dowdied") into the fruit so it absorbs the juices.

Pluck: heart, liver, and lungs. Pluck from calves and lambs is considered best. Pluck Stew was served to helpers at butchering time.

Ramp: a wild leek, a relative of the onion.

Sack: a type of wine imported from Spain and the Canary Islands.

Saleratus: baking soda.

Schnitz: dried apples.

Sippets: toast points or small pieces of fried bread; eaten with soup.

Spider: a cast-iron frying pan with long legs that hold it above the coals on the hearth.

> Moderate oven: 350° F.
> Moderate hot oven: 375° F.
> Soft ball stage: 238° F.
> Slow oven: 325° F.
> Hot oven: 375° to 400° F.

SOUPS & STEWS

Sarah Josepha Hale lists Mock Turtle Soup, Currie Soup, Veal Soup, White Soup, Pigeon Soup and Vegetable Soup in her 1841 compendium. Some of the directions may strike the modern reader as odd, such as the directive under White Soup to "if it is liked, add the best part of the gristles."

Nuts and leaves sometimes went into the stew pot.

SEMINOLE STEW
--The Carolina Housewife, or House and Home (1847)

Take a squirrel, cut it up and put it on to boil. When the soup is nearly done add to it one pint of picked hickory-nuts [that is, the meats picked from the shells] and a spoonful of parched and powdered sassafras leaves — or the tender top of a pine tree, which gives a very aromatic flavor to the soup.

Missouri pioneers dined on jerky, pemmican (jerky pounded with dried berries), Johnnycake, ash cake, pea soup and Basic Stew.

BASIC STEW
--Missouri Department of Conservation

1 meaty soup bone such as beef shank
salt
assorted vegetables (wild garlic, carrots, potatoes,
    onions, celery, tomatoes, etc.)
chopped game meat (optional)

Put soup bone in a stew pot or Dutch oven with 8 to 10 cups cold water. Bring to a boil. Reduce heat, simmer for several hours. Remove bone and dice any meat. Return meat to pot. Add vegetables — whole, chopped or sliced. Simmer one hour or as long as you like, replacing liquid as it evaporates. Season with salt, pepper, bay leaves and/or garlic. If elk or deer meat is available, chop some and throw it in. You can't hurt it. Yield: 8 servings.

SOUPS & STEWS

The soup of choice for Utah's hardy pioneers was St. Jacob's:

ST. JACOB'S SOUP
--Utah State Office of Education

¼ pound bacon, sliced
1 pound potatoes, cut in large dice
¼ pound onions, peeled and chopped
1½ cups (or a 14-ounce can) tomatoes

Dice bacon finely and cook until brown but not crisp. Cook potatoes and onions in water to cover until tender. Add bacon with some of the drippings. Add tomatoes. Simmer 10 minutes. Season to taste with salt and pepper.Yield: 4 servings.

Traditional eighteenth-century soups in Ferne Shelton's *Southern Appalachian Mountain Cookbook* (1964) include Potato Soup, Vegetable Soup (flavored with a soup bone), Mountain Stew (not unlike Brunswick Stew), Irish Stew (lamb, turnips, etc.), Fish Stew (with trout or flounder), and Old Stone Stew (like Brunswick but with stew beef rather than a stewing hen).

Catawba County Historic Society

SOUPS & STEWS

Brunswick Stew is a regional dish that appears regularly in Southern cookbooks including *Common Sense in the Household* (1873).

One version of Brunswick Stew traces its origins to Brunswick County, Virginia. Tradition has it that the dish was created in 1828 by an African-American chef, "Uncle" Jimmy Matthews. While serving as camp cook during a hunting expedition, Matthews shot squirrels, combined them with onions, dry bread and other ingredients, and made dinner. The tasty dish caught on. Simmered outdoors over an open fire, it was often served during Fourth of July celebrations.

Another version was first prepared on St. Simons Island, Georgia, in 1898. This version is usually cooked for less time and left chunkier than the Virginia version. Some cooks start with a whole hog's head.

The Booyah or Booya of Wisconsin, Minnesota and Indiana is a similar dish. Reputed to be Belgian in origin, Booya is served at family reunions, church picnics and other community events. Chicken, beef, corn, lima beans and other fresh vegetables meld their flavors.

Some fans find the combination of ingredients romantic:

> Potato was deep in the dark under ground
> Tomato, above in the light;
> The little Tomato was ruddy and round,
> The little Potato was white.
> And redder and redder she rounded above.
> And paler and paler he grew,
> And neither suspected a mutual love,
> Till they met in a Brunswick stew.
> --from "The Tryst," by John Banister Tabb
> Haw Branch Plantation, Amelia, VA.

SOUPS & STEWS

Many variations of Brunswick Stew have been created since 1828, including a stew topped with cornmeal dumplings. The following comes direct from Brunswick County where the visitors' center displays an iron pot outside:

First catch your chickens, clean and cut them.
And in an iron pot you put them.
And water nearly to the top
And in it salt and pepper drop;
Boil slowly. Your tomatoes peel;
Put in a shin or so of veal;
And for the flavor bear in mind,
A chunk of middling with the rind.
Next some onions you throw in,
The young and tender skin,
And butter beans do not forget;
And what is more important yet;
The corn, but do not be too fast,
For you must cut and add it last;
For better than the flour you'll find it'll do
To give some thickness to the stew.
Some lemon peel cut very thin
May then be added and stirred in,
And ere it's taken from the fire
Give it a dash of Worcestershire,
And soon you will hear its praises ring,
This is a dish fit for a king.
   --Virginia Woodroof, 1930

SOUPS & STEWS

The Virginia version combines equal parts squirrel and pork. The Georgia version combines chicken and pork.

GEORGIA-STYLE BRUNSWICK STEW

> **4 tablespoons bacon drippings**
> **1 large onion, diced**
> **1 pound chicken, cooked and diced**
> **1 pound pork, cooked and diced**
> **4 large diced potatoes, parboiled**
> **2 cans butter beans**
> **3 cans cream-style corn**
> **black pepper, salt and hot sauce to taste**

Cook onion in bacon drippings until transparent. Put into a stew pot with remaining ingredients. Cover and simmer, stirring occasionally to keep from sticking. When heated through, adjust seasonings. Serve. Yield: 6 servings.

Photo by Wayne Erbsen

Hart's Square Village

SOUPS & STEWS

Soup is both nourishing and restorative. Scots-Irish pioneers doted on Scotch Broth and Cock-A-Leekie. Italians dished up *Pasta e Fagioli* (pasta and beans) and *Zuppa di Pesce* (fish soup). Pioneers of German origin prepared steaming pots of *Hirschbrust* (Venison Stew) and *Linsensuppe* (Lentil Soup with leek, parsnip, turnip, bacon and pork neck bones). Scandinavians enjoyed *Arter Med Flask* (yellow pea soup with pork) and *Fruktsoppa* (a cold soup of dried fruit). Basque sheepherders sat down to a soup of chickpeas and potatoes, while Portuguese dairy farmers in California favored *Caldo Verde* (potato and kale soup).

Soups can be made from fresh fish, flesh or fowl, vegetables, water or milk, and from odds and ends of all. Have always on hand whole and ground spices, sweet herbs, celery-seed, parsley, onions, carrots and turnips; rice, barley, tapioca, corn starch and flour to thicken and enrich.
--*Country Cooking* (Kansas, 1907)

STEWED CATFISH
--Marion Harland, *Common Sense in the Household*, 1893

Skin, clean, and cut off the horribly homely heads. Sprinkle with salt, to remove any muddy taste they may have contracted from the flats or holes in which they have fed, and let them lie in a cool place for an hour or so. Then put them into a saucepan, cover with cold water, and stew very gently for from half to three-quarters of an hour, according to their size. Add a chopped shallot or button-onion, a bunch of chopped parsley, a little pepper, a large tablespoonful of butter, a tablespoonful of flour mixed to a paste with cold water; boil up once, take the fish carefully, and lay in a deep dish. Boil up the gravy once more, and strain over the fish. Send to table in a covered dish.

SOUPS & STEWS

Add a few vegetables to a Mess of Greens, and you have vegetable soup. Many pioneer soups were based on dried beans, especially peas. Shaker cooks at Sabbathday Lake in Maine served dishes such as Swedish meat balls, chicken roasted with fresh tarragon, and split pea soup made with yellow split peas.

SHAKER PEA SOUP

> 3 slices bacon or fat back, chopped
> 1 large onion, chopped
> 5 cups water
> 1½ cups yellow split peas
> 1 teaspoon dried thyme
> 1 teaspoon dried savory or sage
> salt to taste

Fry bacon or fat back in Dutch oven. When nearly cooked, add onion. Stir and cook until onion is lightly browned. Add water, then remaining ingredients. Bring to a boil. Then reduce heat, cover, and simmer for about an hour and a quarter, or until peas are soft. Yield: 6 servings.

Photo by Fernand L. Chandonnet

SOUPS & STEWS

Nothing beats beef stew on a cold, snowy night. Served with fresh bread or quick bread, it's heaven.

BEEF STEW
As it simmers on the hearth or stovetop, Beef Stew fills the kitchen with delightful aromas. If there are bell peppers and tomatoes in the garden, add one of each, chopped.

2 pounds beef stew meat, cubed
¼ cup flour
¼ cup oil
4 cups water or beef stock
2 large onions, chopped
2 garlic cloves, chopped (optional)
1 bay leaf
2 sprigs thyme (optional)
2 teaspoons salt
freshly ground black pepper to taste
1 sweet potato, peeled and cut into 1-inch chunks
6 medium potatoes, trimmed and quartered
6 medium carrots or parsnips, peeled and cut into
    1-inch chunks
¼ cup cold water
¼ cup cornstarch

Coat beef cubes with flour. In a Dutch oven, brown meat in hot oil. Add the water, chopped onion, garlic, bay leaf, salt and pepper. Bring to boiling. Then reduce heat, cover and simmer one and a half to 2 hours or until meat is tender. Add potatoes and carrots. Simmer about another hour or until vegetables are tender. Add bell pepper and tomato if using. A cup of leftover peas or frozen peas may also be added.
In a small bowl, combine cold water and cornstarch. Stir into stew. Cook and stir until mixture thickens, about 5 minutes. Remove bay leaf before serving. Yield: 8 servings.

SOUPS & STEWS

Dumplings are an ancient peasant dish—a simple way to add substance to stew. In spring, Scots-Irish cooks made green dumplings, speckled with dandelion and nettle leaves or hawthorn buds. Made of biscuit or bread dough, dumplings often serve as a meat substitute. Dumplings were served by the pioneer cook with raspberry vinegar, melted butter, or gravy. Oatmeal dumplings made with equal parts of wheat flour and oatmeal, seasoned with onion, are delicious atop beef or lamb stew.

Chicken and Dumplings is a favorite Texas pioneer dish, often made with prairie chickens. The Pickett House Restaurant at Heritage Village in Woodville, Texas, serves Chicken and Dumplings as well as biscuits and cobbler.

BUTTERMILK DUMPLINGS
Recycle leftover Beef Stew by baking biscuits on top. This creates crusty dumplings.

½ recipe Beef Stew
Biscuits:
1½ cups sifted flour
1½ teaspoons baking powder
½ teaspoon salt
¼ teaspoon baking soda
¼ cup butter or canola oil
½ cup buttermilk

Combine dry ingredients. Cut in butter until mixture resembles coarse meal. Add buttermilk. Stir until dough holds together. Transfer dough to lightly floured or cornmeal-covered surface. Knead 8 to 10 times. Roll dough to half-inch thickness. Cut with floured cutter into rounds. Preheat oven to 425°. Heat stew until bubbly; put into an ovenproof casserole or skillet. Place biscuits on top. Bake at 425° for 12 to 15 minutes. Yield: 4 servings.

SOUPS & STEWS

Most of the first companies of Mormon settlers originated in New England. Later companies hailed from Europe, Wales, Spain and even Australia. Fresh-caught trout, rolled in cornmeal and fried golden in bacon fat, was a favorite main dish for Western pioneers. When chickens were brought across the plains about 1847, this became a standard Mormon soup.

VELVET CHICKEN SOUP
   --Ensign, July 1972

> **3 to 4 pound whole chicken**
> **3 quarts cold water**
> **1 tablespoon salt**
> **6 peppercorns**
> **1 onion, chopped**
> **2 tablespoons chopped celery**
> **2 cups rich milk or cream**
> **1 tablespoon cornstarch**
> **1 tablespoon butter**
> **salt and pepper**
> **2 eggs, well beaten**

One day before serving: Cut chicken into pieces. Put in kettle with cold water and salt. Cover. Bring to a boil, then reduce heat and simmer until tender.

Remove from heat. Remove chicken from bones, and put aside for sandwiches or Chicken Pot Pie. Return bones to stock and add peppercorns, onion and celery. Simmer until stock is reduced to 1 quart. Strain. Cool. Remove all fat.

Day of serving: Add milk or cream to defatted stock. Bring just to a boil. Mix cornstarch with a little cold water until smooth. Stir into stock with butter. Season to taste. In a bowl, beat eggs with a little additional milk. Pour 1 cup soup over egg mixture, to warm. Then pour egg mixture into soup. Stir constantly for 2 minutes. Serve hot with croutons. Yield: 6 servings.

SOUPS & STEWS

This dish will be recognized by the discerning as a variant on Cheese Rabbit or Welsh Rabbit or Cheese Rarebit. It is considered Sunday night supper in New Hampshire. Sometimes it's called Ring-Tum Diddy. The cheese used is what's known as "cracker barrel" or "mouse trap" — the oldest Cheddar you can find. Consider it domestic fondue.

RUM TUM TIDDY
   —Corinne Woodbury manuscript, courtesy Dave Woodbury

   2 tablespoons butter
   1 tablespoon flour
   1 cup tomato soup
   ½ can beer
   1 teaspoon salt
   1 teaspoon Worcestershire sauce
   2 cups grated or cubed cheese
   1 beaten egg
   a pinch of soda
   toast or crackers

Melt butter in the top of a double boiler. Stir in flour and mix well. Add tomato soup and beer, salt, Worcestershire and cheese. Stir until cheese is melted. Add beaten egg. Cook until thickened. Just before removing from stove to serve, add pinch of soda. Serve on squares of toast or on crisp crackers.
   Yield: 6 servings.

CHURNING BUTTER

One of womankind's greatest inventions, butter, is made by agitating cream until it emulsifies. This task is best accomplished with a churn—typically a vessel of wood or glazed ceramic. Late in the nineteenth century, churns became metal in an effort to make them both larger and more sanitary. Churns could hold as little as three pints of cream or as much as 60 gallons. Some of the larger ones resemble early washing machines. After bits of butter form, they must be collected and "worked" to remove the last traces of buttermilk. Lastly, butter was formed into balls with wooden paddles, decorated with stamps or pressed into carved molds.

Churning was a laborious chore for the housewife. The butter churn might be a tall wooden vessel, a pottery container, a glass jar with a metal cover and dasher or a square contraption with its own base. Mail order catalogs from the late 1800s illustrate several different types—all operated with female biceps.

BUTTER
This modern recipe takes only 20 minutes.

> **4 cups heavy cream**
> **1½ teaspoons coarse salt**
> **2 cups ice water**
> **a chilled bowl**

In a blender on medium speed, mix cream and salt until grainy milk curds begin to form, 8 to 10 minutes.

Pour milk curds through a strainer. Discard liquid. Transfer solids to a chilled bowl.

Pour half a cup of ice water over curds and press out any residual liquid (whey) with the side of a rubber bowl scraper. Drain water when it gets cloudy. Then add new ice water, half a cup at a time. Continue to press out whey and drain. Repeat until water stays clear. Yield: 12 ounces.

CHURNING BUTTER

Library of Congress

A 12-acre oasis in Denver, Colorado, the Four Mile Historic Park, offers a class in butter making.

In Appalachia, butter making was done on a very small scale. Hence the churns held less. They took the form of lap churns or lap troughs, with the butter worked by a "clasher."

SWEET BUTTER
To have sweet butter in dog days, and through the vegetable seasons, send stone pots to honest, neat, and trusty dairy people, and procure it packed down in May, and let them be brought in the night, or cool rainy mornings, covered with a clean cloth wet in cold water, and partake of no heat from the horse, and set the pots in the coldest part of your cellar, or in the ice-house.
--Amelia Simmons, 1796

They that have no other meat gladly bread and butter eat. --Clarke, *Paroemiologia*, 1639

FROM SNOUT TO TAIL

Hog butchering was usually accomplished after the first frost. Into the late 1800s, slaughtering took place both on farms and in towns like Portsmouth, New Hampshire. The process took days. One  day was allotted to cutting and salting the raw flesh, and another to trying and straining tallow and lard. Methods of preservation included dry salting, soaking in brine or "pickle" and smoking. *The Cook Not Mad, or Rational Cookery* (1830) gives directions for pickling 100 pounds of beef "to keep a year." Preservatives for each barrel of meat are 3 quarts salt, 6 ounces saltpeter and 3 cups molasses.

When the barrels of salted meat were sealed, housewives began making sausage. They cleaned intestines carefully, and filled them with cut or shredded meat seasoned with sage. The links were smoked in the chimney. Bulk sausage was formed into patties, fried, then stored in pottery crocks and  covered with melted fat. At the Sauer-Beckmann Farm in Texas, pioneers made blood sausage, liver sausage and headcheese.

Hams were sometimes pickled briefly, then dried and aged in an attic, chimney or smokehouse. Some cuts were set aside to be eaten fresh, and some were shared with neighbors—who would reciprocate when they killed their own hogs or beef.

FROM SNOUT TO TAIL

To Make Sausage Meat
--Sarah Josepha Hale, *The Good Housekeeper* (1841)
Chop two pounds of lean with one of fat pork very fine —
mix with this meat five teaspoons of salt, seven of powdered
sage, two of black pepper, and one of cloves. You can add a
little rosemary, if you like it.

Prepared from heads, feet and ears, Souse and Head
Cheese were next. The latter is much like the former except
that vinegar is omitted. Souse was sliced and browned in the
oven. Head Cheese was served cold with mustard pickles.
Salted pork and corned beef were usually served in a
variation on boiled dinner — meat and vegetables simmered
in a pot over the fire, or beef, pork, beets, carrots and turnips
in a universal stew that might be eaten three times a day. The
majority of the meat put down in fall had been consumed by
late spring or early summer.

Sausage is an ancient dish reportedly produced from
chopped and seasoned pork in 7000 B.C. in the Far East and
Egypt. New England sailors made sausage from dolphin
when pork was not available, and Alaskans often create it by
combining pork with elk, moose or bear. Specialty sausages
include andouille, bratwurst, chorizo, kielbasa and morta-
della.

FROM SNOUT TO TAIL

Because there are only two hams to a pig, they were regularly saved for special occasions like New Year's. For boiling ham, William Byrd, one of Virginia's first settlers, favored a mixture of milk and water. Byrd recorded his cooking directions on a flyleaf of his Bible at his residence, Westover, about 1674:

BYRD'S HAM
"To eat ye Ham in Perfection steep it in Half Milk and Half Water for 36 hours, and then having brought the water to a boil put ye Ham therein and let it simmer, not boil, for 4 to 5 hours according to Size of ye Ham for simmering brings ye salt out and boiling drives it in."

Ham is the centerpiece of holiday feasts at the George Ranch Historic Park in Richmond, Texas. The ham shares the table with roast turkey, beans, rolls, doughnuts and pecan pie. In the Llano Estacado region of West Texas and eastern New Mexico, the holiday table is spread with pheasant, venison, and veal as well as winter greens.

FROM SNOUT TO TAIL

VIRGINIA BAKED HAM

> 1 small, lean ham, about 7 pounds
> 1 tablespoon baking soda
> 1 quart sweet (i.e., not hard) apple cider
> 2 tablespoons brown sugar
> 1 beaten egg
> ½ teaspoon ground cinnamon
> about 4 tablespoons bread crumbs
> ½ teaspoon celery seed
> 10 peppercorns
> 6 to 12 whole cloves

Wash ham thoroughly. Sprinkle with soda, rubbing it into the surface. Rinse in cold water. Place in a deep kettle with the celery seed, cinnamon, peppercorns and cider. Add boiling water to just cover the ham. Simmer until very tender — about 25 minutes per pound.

Remove boiled ham from kettle. Drain, reserving any juices that drip out for soup stock. When the ham is cool enough to handle, peel off skin. With a sharp knife, mark surface in one-inch squares. Sprinkle with sugar. Brush with the beaten egg, cover with the bread crumbs, patting them into the egg so they adhere. Insert whole cloves at intervals, and bake in a 450° oven until brown. Serve with White Sauce. Yield: 12 servings.

FROM SNOUT TO TAIL

Photo by Wayne Erbsen

Popular from Alabama to Texas is the dish known as Sawmill Gravy. Or Country Gravy. Or Sausage Gravy. It's not for the faint of heart—or stomach.

SAUSAGE GRAVY
1 pound bulk sausage
4 tablespoons lard or
shortening
⅓ cup flour
3 cups milk (about)
crumbled sage (optional)
salt and pepper to taste
biscuits

Cook sausage over medium heat, stirring and breaking up with wooden spoon. When browned, remove to a plate and allow to drain.

Add lard to skillet—or use just the sausage drippings. Stir in flour. When mixture bubbles, gradually add milk. Season to taste with sage, salt and pepper. Return sausage to skillet. If gravy is too pasty, reduce with a bit more milk. Serve hot over split biscuits. Sliced tomatoes make a good side.

Serves 6 to 8.

"In the Spring are several sorts of Herbs, a corn-sallet, violets, sorrell, purslaine—all of which are very good and wholesome and by the English used for sallets and in broth."
--Leonard Calvert, Governor of Maryland, writing to his brother,1636

FROM SNOUT TO TAIL

When sausage was unavailable, Southern cooks made a similar dish with salt pork, seasoning with onion instead of sage.

SALT PORK IN MILK GRAVY

1 pound salt pork
cornmeal
1 onion, chopped

Slice salt pork thinly. Dip slices in boiling water. Drain, then cover with cornmeal. Brown slowly in a skillet until cooked through. Remove salt pork to a plate. Add onion and saute until golden. Then proceed as above to make milk gravy. Serve with cornbread and a mess of greens.

A garnish helps to make a meat dish more attractive— both to the eye and the palate.

FRIED APPLES
--The Century Cook Book, 1895
Cut slices one half inch thick across the apple, giving circles. Do not remove the skin or core. Saute in butter or drippings until tender, but not soft enough to lose form. Serve fried apples on the same dish with pork chops as garnish.

FROM SNOUT TO TAIL

CAROLINA COUNTRY STYLE RIBS
-- National Pork Board

> 1½ to 2 pounds boneless country-style ribs
> 2 cups apple cider vinegar
> 1 cup cold water
> 2 tablespoons vegetable oil
> 2 tablespoons molasses or
> ¼ cup firmly packed brown sugar
> 1 tablespoon Kosher salt
> 1½ teaspoons red pepper flakes
> ½ teaspoon cayenne pepper

Place ribs in a large bowl or sealed plastic bag. Set aside. In a 4-cup glass measure, stir together vinegar, water, oil, molasses, salt, red pepper flakes and cayenne pepper until salt is dissolved. Remove ½ cup marinade; reserve. Add remaining marinade to ribs; seal bag or cover bowl and marinated for 4 to 6 hours in the refrigerator. When ready to cook, remove ribs from marinade, and discard marinade.

Grilling: Prepare medium-hot fire. Grill ribs over indirect heat for 50 to 60 minutes or until pork is tender and the internal temperature reaches 160° F on a meat thermometer. During last 15 minutes of grilling time, baste ribs twice with reserved marinade mixture. Yield: 6 servings.

Use tidbits of ham to flavor black-eyed peas, grits, cornbread, scones, red rice and jambalaya. Tidbits can also fill an omelet or garnish a green salad. Use small country ham slices to fill biscuits slathered with pear preserves, mustard or pepper jelly.

The excellency of hogs is fatness, of men virtue. --1736

55

DISSECTING THE PIG

"Fried hog's feet were nearly the best of the hog killing. After boiling tender, the feet were split lengthwise in half, rolled in sifted cornmeal, salted and peppered. And fried crisp in plenty of boiling hot fat. Served with hot biscuits and stewed sun-dried peaches, along with strong coffee, brown and fragrant, they made a supper or breakfast one could rejoice in. "
--*Dishes & Beverages of the Old South*, 1913

It was said that the American Indians of the Plains used the buffalo from nose to tail; the tail served as a fly whisk. The same thrift applied to pigs raised by pioneer Americans. As the old saying has it, "Everything was useful but the squeal."

On farms and homesteads, consuming every scrap of the family porker was part of the seasonal cycle of foodstuffs. Ham was just two legs of the delicious beast. Cleaned intestines were valued as sausage casings. Bones were cracked and then boiled for bone butter.

Today's urban dwellers have scant idea how to process intestines or deal with a pig's head. And perhaps we'd rather not learn! Here are a few definitions to clear up questions at the grocery store:

Fat Back: Commercial fat back has been cured with salt as a temporary preservative. It is similar to salt pork but may have streaks of lean that resemble those of bacon. It can be simmered for 20 minutes and eaten on its own. Or use as seasoning for a pot of collards or poke. Fat back is the cut baked for hours with dried beans or black eyed peas; after the bean pot has simmered six hours in the oven, the fat back will be tender enough to spread on bread. Half an ounce of simmered fat back contains about the same calories as a tablespoon of butter or olive oil.

DISSECTING THE PIG

Chitterlings or chitlins: The small intestines, usually fried in deep fat. The word comes from a Middle English term originally describing either entrails or souse. An African-American cook in Oakland, California, tells me her family insists that she cook chitlins at least once a year. She agrees to cook them--in a pot in the back yard.

Ham: The upper part of a hog's hind leg, cured by salting, smoking, etc. The butt, or upper half, is meatier but more difficult to carve.

Hock: The bony joint corresponding to the human ankle. Excellent for soup stock or seasoning.

Jowl Bacon: The meat of a hog's cheeks, cured like bacon, and simmered with greens.

Pork neck bones: A basis for tasty stock; bones add gelatin to the broth if simmered at least 2 hours.

Shoulder: The smoked shoulder is also known as a picnic shoulder. Allow half a pound to a pound per serving.

Shoulder butt: The shoulder butt is a boneless cut from the neck and shoulder. It is also called Boston butt and cottage ham. Sliced, it can be used as bacon. It may also be roasted or simmered or used as stew meat.

Pigs feet: Some like them pickled.

Center ham slice: This cut is efficient for the small family who doesn't need a 10-pound roast beast. Frying is its middle name. But the meaty slice is also eminently suitable for kabobs and grilling.

Country-style ribs: This cut has more meat on it than the typical ribs served as barbecued ribs. These ribs are delicious roasted for two hours at 325°. Add to the pan an onion stuck with cloves. Add a little water to the pan if the drippings begin to scorch.

MEATS & MAIN DISHES

Pioneers consumed almost any meat that moved, from venison to frog. Recent winners at the West Virginia Road Kill Cook-Off include a Venison, Buffalo and Sausage Stew and Pothole Possum Stew. This is a recipe from that event.

SWEET POTATO & POSSUM
--Ashland Daily Tidings, May 23, 2007

**1 dressed opossum
4 cups sweet potato chunks, size of small lemons
melted butter
1 cup light brown sugar
1 tablespoon ground cinnamon**

Day before: Soak possum in cold salted water to remove gamey taste. Refrigerate overnight in water.

Cooking: Drain possum and pat dry. Salt and pepper cavity. Smear all over with melted butter. Dip potato chunks in melted butter, and then roll in a mixture of the sugar and cinnamon. Stuff cavity with potatoes. Bake at 350° until meat is done and potatoes tender, about 2 hours.

The Cook Not Mad, published anonymously in New York State in 1830, included a recipe for stuffing a turkey:

To Stuff a Turkey
Grate a [dry] wheat loaf, one quarter of a pound of butter, one quarter of a pound of salt pork, finely chopped, two eggs, a little sweet marjoram, summer savory, parsley, pepper and salt, if the pork be not sufficient, fill the bird and sew up. The same will answer for all wild fowls.

MEATS & MAIN DISHES

Pioneers on the Oregon Trail made beef, elk or buffalo jerky which kept during hot weather and could be chewed without cooking or simmered into stew.

BEEF JERKY
--Whitman Mission National Historic Site

> **1 flank or London broil or other lean beef**
> **salt and pepper**
> **1 cup soy sauce**
> **aluminum foil**

Cut steak into strips with the grain of the meat. Pour soy sauce into a bowl, and dip strips into it. Lay a piece of foil on an oven rack, and place strips on it. Salt and pepper on both sides. Place the rack into a broiler pan with a sheet of foil under the rack, to catch drips. Bake at 150° for 10 hours. Start at night, and the jerky will be ready for hiking next day.

Sarah Smith, wife of a missionary, crossed the country in 1838 and cooked on the Oregon Trail. She writes in her diary about making buffalo gravy. She also tells of making meat pies and how she improvised for lack of a rolling pin:

"June 30, 1838: ...this afternoon made a couple of pies, chop meat with a butcher knife on the back of a cotton-wood tree which Mr. S peeled off. Rolled the crust with a crooked stick in a whole bark, baked in the tin baker out of doors in the wind but they were good and we have had a good supper."

MEATS & MAIN DISHES

The taste for barbecue drove west with pioneers from Virginia, Missouri and Kansas, where it quickly adopted chilies. Indiana's Conner Prairie Museum consults *The Backcountry Housewife* by Kate Moss and Kathryn Hoffman as one of their sources for pioneer food. Moss and Hoffman note that grilling (barbecuing) was important in daily menus. For instance, *The Virginia Housewife* (1824) contains a recipe for barbecued shoat (a young hog of about 35 pounds on the hoof). Barbecued squirrel was not unknown—although certainly less savory than shoat. Children turned the spit, and juices were caught in a pan on the hearth.

BARBECUE SANDWICHES
--Portal to Texas History, *Hemphill County News* (Texas), August 23, 1940

> **2 pounds beef**
> **2 pounds pork**
> **1 tablespoon chili powder**
> **1 teaspoon white pepper**
> **¼ teaspoon red pepper**
> **1 teaspoon dry mustard**
> **1½ teaspoons salt**
> **¼ cup flour**
> **1½ cups tomato puree or**
> **condensed tomato soup**
> **1½ quarts meat stock**
> **3 large onions, sliced**

Cook meat until tender in enough water to cover. Drain and grind coarsely. Combine seasonings and flour. Add tomato puree and meat stock and cook 5 minutes.

Brown onions lightly in butter or bacon fat, and add to the sauce with the coarsely ground meat. Serve hot on large, round buns. Will fill 3 to 4 dozen buns.

MEATS & MAIN DISHES

Pilau and Cassereau were related pioneer recipes with ancient Arabic and Persian roots. Varying in consistency from soupy to dry, these dishes appear plentifully in Mrs. Stoney's *Carolina Rice Cook Book* (1901). Mrs. Stoney notes in her introduction that "The majority of these receipts have been in constant use for over a century, passing from generation to generation, precious heirlooms." Here is an example:

CASSEREAU
Take a heaping pint of rice cooked as if for dinner, have a fowl boiled, have a rich tomato sauce. Mix the rice and sauce together, adding a heaping tablespoonful of butter, salt and pepper; put a layer of rice in the bottom of your dish, then add the fowl, cut up, and a few pieces of ham or bacon, and then put the rest of the rice on top; bake [at 350°] until brown [and heated through].

Photo by Fernand L. Chandonnet

MEATS & MAIN DISHES

Pork and apples go together like peanut butter and jelly.

PORK & APPLE DINNER
Because beef cattle require extensive pasture while pigs can forage for themselves, Eastern pioneers ate more pork than beef.

Cooking apples include the Grimes Golden, Pippin, McIntosh, Jonathan, Newton, Rhode Island Greening, Rome Beauty and Stayman. Dried apples may be substituted for fresh apples.

> 1½ pounds lean pork, cut in 1-inch cubes
> 3 tablespoons oil
> 1 cup water or broth
> 1 medium chopped onion
> 1 teaspoon powdered sage
> ¾ teaspoon salt
> ½ cup milk
> ¼ cup flour
> 2 large cooking apples (3 cups sliced)
> 1 tablespoon sugar
> Peel, cored, and slice apples

In Dutch oven, brown pork cubes in hot oil. Add water, onion, sage and salt. Cover and simmer 20 minutes or until meat is tender. Combine milk and flour; stir into pork mixture. Cook, stirring, until mixture is thickened.

Turn half the hot pork mixture into a 2-quart casserole. Place apple slices over meat. Sprinkle with sugar. Top with remaining pork mixture. Bake at 450° for 10 minutes. Reduce heat to 350° and bake 25 minutes more. Serve with rice or buttered egg noodles. Yield: 6 servings.

An Egg today is bettyer than a Hen tomorrow. --1736

MEATS & MAIN DISHES

Salt codfish was a common pioneer foodstuff. In very dry atmospheres, fish can be dried in the air; it is called stockfish. In warmer, more humid New England, it was necessary to use a desiccant — salt — to preserve cod for long-term storage. At the end of the 1800s, fishing communities on the Atlantic boasted acres of "fish flakes" — outdoor drying racks covered with fish drying in the air. One can only imagine the scent of these communities in places like Gloucester, which produced 53 million pounds of salt cod in 1874. The drying process began in the holds of fishing vessels at sea and continued on land. The resultant object looked more like rough-sawn pine than food. Some families preserved oily fish like eels and alewives by smoking them at home. Codfish cakes were a staple of the New England diet, especially for Catholics on Fridays and holy days.

SALT CODFISH

--Mary Ronald, *The Century Cook Book*, 1895

Soak the codfish several hours, changing the water three times. Simmer it for 20 minutes or until it is tender. Take out carefully all the bones. Make a white sauce of one tablespoon each of butter and flour, and one cupful of milk; add to it, off the heat, two beaten yolks. Return to the fire, and stir in one cupful of shredded codfish. Taste to see if it needs seasoning with salt and pepper. Serve it on slices of toast.

PIONEER MENUS

From the plains of Canada to the plains of Texas, from Maine to Iowa, pioneers often joined forces in large projects. They might help one another put up cabins before the first snowfall, and, when fields had been cleared, combine their labor in a barn raising. While the men sweated and heaved, the women put together a lavish spread.

Today at the Lang Pioneer Village in Keene, Ontario, or the Tillamook County Pioneer Museum in Tillamook, Oregon, special events include occasions such as a Snowflake Festival, a demonstration of rawhide braiding or recitations of cowboy poetry. As in the past, these occasions call for lots of hearty eats.

FOOD FOR A BARN RAISING
> 115 lemon pies
> 500 doughnuts
> 15 large cakes
> 3 gallons apple sauce
> 3 gallons rice pudding
> 3 gallons cornstarch pudding
> 16 chickens
> 3 hams
> 50 pounds roast beef
> 300 light rolls
> 16 loaves of bread
> red beet pickles and pickled eggs
> 6 pounds prunes, stewed
> 1 large crock stewed raisins
> 5 gallon stone jar white potatoes
> 5 gallon stone jar sweet potatoes

(Meal for 115 men.)   --Saskatchewan Home Economists

PIONEER MENUS

Large Southern gatherings ranged from hog butchering to weddings to muster days and election days. Shucking corn, threshing parties and quilting bees were social occasions, too—especially for young folks taking the measure of potential mates.

From Vermont to Virginia, when pioneer housewives hosted quilting bees, shucking bees or harvests, they raided their pantries or root cellars for the best preserves and pickles. "Seven sweets and seven sours" sums up the delights of the resulting cooperative feast.

Gingerbread was commonly served on muster days and election days. Strawberry festivals and ice cream socials were often held to raise money for church and civic groups. Church fairs or "sociables" held in winter featured chowders, pumpkin pies and doughnuts. Pies, cakes and box lunches were auctioned.

A HEARTY BREAKFAST

Photo by Wayne Erbsen

Brewis is a breakfast basic made from dry bread. It is an ancient dish; its first written mention dates from 1520. It was originally hard bread soaked in water, then boiled. Usually pieces of fish were added to complete the recipe. The term derives from the word "broth," so often the bread was soaked in broth in which meat had cooked. In the film "Babette's Feast," the cook prepares Alebrod—bread simmered with ale to make a thick pottage.

There were no bread preservatives until the 20th century, although loaves containing honey, butter and/or eggs would keep a little longer than bread without. In pioneer days, bread was usually baked once a week, 10 or 12 loaves at a time. Bread that was slightly dried out could be sliced and used to prepare French Toast or Sippets. Any loaves that dried out completely before they were consumed were recycled in dishes like Brewis, or made into crumbs that could be used to stuff poultry or whole fish or used to thicken stew. Bread crumbs were also recycled in steamed dessert puddings.

Nothing was wasted; if the bread had begun to mold in green spots, it could be fed to pigs or hens. As the Vermont proverb goes, "Never throw away food that will make a pig open his mouth."

A HEARTY BREAKFAST

Bread and milk was a common country supper dish with minimal prep—just chunks of fresh bread in a dish, covered with milk. Brewis is a little more complex and richer, but easily prepared on the open hearth. Rich foods were welcome to pioneers who had to endure hard physical labor and exposure to the elements.

BREWIS

> **2 cups dry Brown Bread, or Graham Bread**
> **1½ cups milk**
> **½ cup cream**
> **1½ tablespoons butter**
> **¼ teaspoon salt**

Break the brown bread in bite-size pieces. Scald the milk, cream and butter together. Add the salt and dried brown bread. Stir. Let soak 5 minutes. Simmer over a very low flame until milk is absorbed. Serve with a pitcher of cream. Yield: 4 servings.

A HEARTY BREAKFAST

FTER his retirement to Mount Vernon, George Washington rose early to read or write for an hour. Then he breakfasted on three hoe cakes with honey and butter and three cups of tea (without cream).

The modern man, who sits at a desk all day, might look askance at a T-bone on his breakfast plate, but the pioneer needed fuel. Hot biscuits spread with spicy Apple Butter or Cider Jelly, eggs, fried steak, pork chops, fried apples, apple or pumpkin pie, apple turnovers, fried pies, hash brown potatoes, Red Flannel Hash, steaming grits, gravy, pancakes, buckwheat cakes, eel, kedgeree, sausage patties put down in a crock in November, rashers of bacon, venison stew, scrapple, fried ham. These are some of the delights the pioneer enjoyed for breakfast before going out to wield the axe, hoe the beans or take the cows to pasture. He may, in fact, have already put in several hours milking the cows and mucking out the barn before coming in to breakfast. Some of that fuel might come from Indian Slapjacks, a cornmeal griddle cake.

A HEARTY BREAKFAST

INDIAN SLAPJACK
--Amelia Simmons, *American Cookery* (Hartford, 1796)

One quart of milk, 1 pint of indian meal, 4 eggs, 4 spoons of flour, little salt, beat together, baked on gridles [sic], or fry in a dry pan, or baked in a pan which has been rub'd with suet, lard, or butter.

Slapjack is a version of Cornmeal Mush, enriched with eggs, and fried. Ash Cakes, Polenta and Hush Puppies are also variants on Cornmeal Mush or Hasty Pudding -- a mainstay of pioneer diet. The first written New England recipe was supplied by Joel Barlow of Connecticut. Barlow's 1793 rhyme describes the housewife strewing cornmeal into boiling water. The mixture becomes so thick that a manly arm takes over the stirring. Then the pudding must be properly served: spoonfuls dropped into a bowl of milk until each surfaces like a "soft island." Raised on the dish, Barlow allowed as how all his bones were "made of Indian corn."

CORNMEAL MUSH/HASTY PUDDING
--Jenny June's *American Cookery Book* (1866)

Boil water, mix in a little salt, and then stir in gradually so as to prevent lumping, sufficient corn meal to thicken it. It should boil at least an hour, and may be eaten with milk, cream and sugar, or butter and syrup, or sugar.

Miss Parloa's New Cookbook (1880) recommends a breakfast menu of fruit (as a first course), followed by oatmeal and cream, baked potatoes, mutton chops, rye muffins, hominy griddle cakes, and coffee, tea or chocolate. "Either oatmeal or hominy should always be served at breakfast," the author says.

A HEARTY BREAKFAST

HASTY PUDDING
-- *New England Cookbook* (1936)

Economical and comforting, Hasty Pudding may be served immediately or held in a double boiler for hours. Foods like this were suitable not only for invalids and toddlers, but for any hungry member of the family—especially those who had lost their teeth.

> **1 cup cornmeal**
> **1½ cups boiling water**
> **½ cup cold water**
> **pinch of salt**

Make a paste of the cornmeal and cold water, stirring until there are no lumps and pour gradually into the salted boiling water. Stir until very thick. Serve hot with sugar and milk. Or place in a double boiler and cook from 2 to 3 hours, stirring frequently. Yield: 4 servings.

FRIED CORNMEAL MUSH

Prepare Hasty Pudding the day before you wish to serve it. Pour into a greased 9x5 inch loaf pan and allow to firm overnight in the refrigerator. When cold, cut into slices half an inch thick and fry on an oiled griddle or in  bacon fat in a skillet. Fry brown on both sides. For breakfast, serve hot with maple syrup. For another time of day, ladle hot spaghetti sauce over the slices. Yield: 4 servings.

A HEARTY BREAKFAST

INDIAN PUDDING

In the eighteen hundreds, Indian Pudding was revived for "Pilgrim Dinners" and continues to be a beloved winter dessert in some New England households. Recipes like this became all the rage with the 1876 Colonial Revival.

Indian Pudding is simply an enriched Cornmeal Mush — or, from another culinary angle — baked Slapjack. It is made with milk as well as water, in the usual proportions of a cup of meal to a quart of milk. Two beaten eggs are added. The mixture is seasoned with butter, brown sugar, nutmeg and cinnamon to taste. Then the pudding is baked in a buttered casserole until golden.

Mrs. Rose Terry Cooke, in the Colonial Revival collection *Hartford Election Cake and Other Receipts* (1889), lists the ingredients as 3 quarts and 1 pint sweet milk; three tablespoons (heaped) of corn meal; 1 teacup molasses; one teaspoon salt; half cup butter; ginger to taste. Cooke suggests this process: "When it begins to crust over stir it all up from the bottom, and add one pint cold milk. Repeat this process every half hour, or oftener if the pudding browns too fast, till the five pints are used, then let it bake till done, six hours at least. Use, when hot, with a sauce of grated or granulated maple sugar, stirred into rich cream." This would create a pudding much lighter in texture than the customary proportions of ingredients.

APPLE INDIAN PUDDING
--from Bridgeport, Connecticut, 1920

Add 3 sweet apples (pared, cored, sliced thin) to the basic Indian Pudding recipe. Spice with a teaspoonful of ginger rather than nutmeg and cinnamon. Mix the batter with 3 cups of the milk. Bake at 300° for 4 hours. Stir in the remaining cup of milk after the first hour. Serve hot or cold, with or without a pitcher of cream. Some modern Yankees serve Indian Pudding with hard sauce or vanilla ice cream.

A HEARTY BREAKFAST

SCRAPPLE

Scrapple is an American original combining Corn-meal Mush with pork liver and scraps. In Pennsylvania and New Jersey, large quantities were cooked up in the yard on pork butchering day. Pennsylvanians call the dish Ponhaus.

At the Tyson McCarter Place, an 1876 homestead in Great Smoky Mountains National Park, a corncrib and smokehouse indicate the foods eaten. Hogs, corn, rye, wheat, peaches and apples were grown and combined. Family menus featured pickled peaches as well as Scrapple.

2 pigs knuckles
½ pound lean pork or ground pork
1 onion, stuck with whole cloves to taste
4 cups water

Day 1: Simmer all ingredients 3 hours. Cool. Remove bones and cloves.

Day 2: Use some of broth to make basic Hasty Pudding (page 70). Add diced meat, and season with black pepper and sage to taste. Pour into a greased 9x5-inch loaf pan. Chill overnight.

Day 3: Slice, dredge with flour, and fry until crisp.

Silks and satins put out the Kitchen Fire. 1847

A HEARTY BREAKFAST

Below is another recipe which expects the cook to know the basics. Meal is added until the batter "feels right" to the hand holding the wooden spoon. The cook also had to intuit the right size of baking pan and the right temperature. As many of you know, the experienced cook can smell when something is done—although use of a toothpick confirms the nose.

KATE'S CORN BREAD
--Johnson manuscript, begun 1867

> **1 pint sour milk or buttermilk**
> **2 eggs**
> **not quite a teaspoonful of soda**
> **1 tablespoon flour**
> **Indian meal**

PICKLED PEACHES
--Tennessee Home & Farm Bureau

> **4 cups sugar**
> **2 cups vinegar**
> **24 small whole peaches**
> **4 sticks cinnamon**
> **1 teaspoon whole cloves**
> **1 teaspoon salt**

Photo by Wayne Erbsen

Boil all ingredients except peaches for 5 minutes. Add peaches. Strain out cloves if desired. Simmer 15 minutes or until fruit is tender but not mushy. Place in hot sterile jars and seal. Yield: 3 to 4 quarts.

A HEARTY BREAKFAST

I am a big fan of Corned Beef Hash. I am also a big fan of Red Flannel Hash — which my maternal grandmother had down to a science. The browned crusty bits are the creme de la creme.

My method is to simmer or low-boil halved potatoes until almost tender. During the last couple of minutes of cooking, add diced onion. Drain well. When the potatoes are cool enough to handle, dice into half-inch cubes. (This step may be done the day before.) When you are close to serving, begin by browning the onions and potato first. Then add remaining ingredients. You may use beef broth, aspic, bacon fat or potato cooking water in lieu of cream.

RED FLANNEL HASH

Red Flannel Hash is popular all over New England, where it is generally employed as a tasty method of stretching corned beef and potatoes leftover from a New England Boiled Dinner.

6 medium beets, cooked and peeled
4 medium potatoes, cooked
3 tablespoons butter
1 tablespoon cream
1 cup chopped corned beef or leftover roast beef
salt and pepper to taste

Chop the potatoes and beets into rough cubes of about half an inch. Mix with the meat, and season with salt and pepper. Place two tablespoons butter in a frying pan, add the mixture and moisten with a little hot water. Cook slowly in a covered pan until heated through. When nearly ready to serve, add the cream mixed with the remaining butter. Brown quickly, flip to brown the bottom and serve very hot.

Yield: 4 servings.

A HEARTY BREAKFAST

Some observers thought Americans ate too much meat. One of them was Sarah Josepha Hale (1788-1879): "During childhood and early youth, the breakfast and supper should consist principally of bread and milk, ripe fruits and vegetable food; it will be sufficient to allow a portion of animal food with the dinner [i.e., the noon meal]."

Hale approved of Buckwheat Cakes in the morning. The batter, which included yeast, was allowed to rise overnight in a cool place. Similar cakes were made with rye in some regions. In his book, *America Eats* (1989), William Woys Weaver shows wonderful photos of spouted, stoneware batter pitchers which were set by the hearth in the evening, ready to prepare breakfast the following sunrise. If the fire grew hot during the night, these yeasted batters sometimes overflowed.

RYE CAKES

These hearty flapjacks or pancakes are popular from Maine to Tennessee. Serve with maple syrup.

**1 cup all-purpose flour
1 cup rye flour
1 egg
⅓ cup molasses
1 cup sour milk or buttermilk
1 teaspoon baking soda**

Sift the flours together. Beat the egg in a bowl, mix with the molasses. Dissolve soda in sour milk, and then stir into egg mixture. Combine this with the flours to form a stiff batter. Drop teaspoonfuls of the butter onto a greased griddle or into deep hot fat and fry until brown. Yield: 4 servings.

Time is a herb that cures all Diseases. --1738

A HEARTY BREAKFAST

The following breakfast recipe in rhyme was contributed to *The Woman Suffrage Cook Book* (1886) by Elizabeth Cady Stanton. "Thickened milk" means White Sauce. The salted cod fish would have been soaked in fresh water overnight, drained, covered with water again, and simmered until tender.

BREAKFAST DISH

Cut smoothly from a wheaten loaf
Ten slices, good and true,
And brown them nicely, o'er the coals,
As you for toast would do.

Prepare a pint of thickened milk,
Some cod-fish shredded small;
And have on hand six hard-boiled eggs,
Just right to slice withal.

Moisten two pieces of the bread,
And lay them in a dish,
Upon them slice a hard-boiled egg,
Then scatter o'er with fish.

And for a seasoning you will need
Of pepper just one shake,
Then spread above the milky juice,
And this one layer make.

And thus, five times, bread, fish and egg,
Or bread and egg and fish,
Then place one egg upon the top,
To crown this breakfast dish.

A HEARTY BREAKFAST

 OTHING beats a biscuit hot from the oven. Except maybe two biscuits. Please pass the honey, Honey.

BASIC BISCUITS
Old time cooks used a tumbler rim to cut out biscuits. A sharp cutter is best.
2 cups flour
½ teaspoon salt
3 teaspoons baking powder
½ cup lard or butter
¾ cup water or milk

Mix flour, salt and baking powder. Add lard, and cut in with a fork, pastry blender or fingers until it looks like a coarse meal. Gradually work in milk or water, using as little as possible. On a lightly floured surface, roll dough into a rectangle half an inch thick. Use a sharp cutter to form rounds 2 inches across. Knead scraps together, roll and cut. Put biscuits on a lightly greased baking sheet; do not allow to touch. Bake at 450° for 12 to 15 minutes. Yield: about 12 biscuits.

Biscuit Variations:
• Add 2 tablespoons finely snipped fresh chives and ⅓ cup of grated sharp Cheddar cheese.
• Use whole wheat flour, grated Parmesan cheese and finely chopped rosemary to taste.
• Add ½ cup finely chopped onion and 2 tablespoons chopped parsley.
• Add 2 tablespoons chopped fresh dill and 1 teaspoon celery seed.
• Add ¾ cup cooked sweet potato, mashed.
• Add 1 cup room-temperature mashed potatoes.
• Cheddar & Black Pepper Biscuits: Add 1 cup grated sharp Cheddar and ½ teaspoon freshly grated black pepper.

A HEARTY BREAKFAST

APPLE SHORTCAKE

Make Basic Biscuits, adding ¼ cup of sugar with the dry ingredients. Slice hot biscuits in half. Stack with sweetened applesauce. Serve with whipped cream or a pitcher of sweetened heavy cream.

APPLE FRITTERS

--Adapted from *The Woman's World Fruit Book*, 1928.

Apple Fritters are said to date back to the Vikings. The pioneer housewife served them at breakfast or as a dessert when Sauerbraten was the main dish. Fry about 4 minutes, or until brown on the outside and done in the center.

1 cup flour
¼ teaspoon salt
2 eggs, separated
1 tablespoon olive oil
1 teaspoon baking powder
½ cup milk
4 apples, pared, cored, and sliced

Sift into a bowl the flour, salt and baking powder. Make a hollow in the center, drop into this the yolks of eggs, the oil and just enough milk to moisten the flour. Beat until entirely free from lumps, add remaining milk and the egg whites beaten until stiff. Dip into the batter slices of apple, which have been cored and pared, and cook golden brown in deep hot fat (375°). Drain on unglazed paper, dust with confectioners' sugar and serve with slice of cut lemon or with a sweet sauce. Serves six.

GOOD BREADS

AKING a good loaf of bread was long considered a test of a homemaker's skill. Even unmarried homemakers like the poet Emily Dickinson prided themselves on their baking. Among Emily's specialties were breads, gingerbread and Black Cake (a very dark fruit cake). Petite, reclusive Emily also found it handy to dive into an empty flour barrel in the pantry if guests she did not wish to see knocked at the door.

Delicious "thirded breads" made with one third rye meal, one third cornmeal and one third oats or wheat flour graced the tables of pioneers in the sixteen hundreds and later. These breads ranged from unleavened crackers to leavened biscuits and loaves. Biscuit dough was sometimes shaped into a flat round to fit the bottom of a Dutch oven or a dish pan and baked that way rather than in individual portions.

DRIED HERB BUTTER

½ c. butter
¼ tsp. sage
½ tsp. basil
½ tsp. tarragon
½ tsp. thyme

Beat together softened butter and dried herbs. Chill. Serve with hot rolls or bread. Substitute fresh herbs when available.

Photo by Wayne Erbsen

GOOD BREADS

HOMEMADE CRACKERS
--Great Smoky Mountains National Park

½ cup quick cooking oats
1⅓ cups all purpose flour
½ cup stone ground whole wheat flour
⅓ cup wheat germ or all purpose flour
1 tablespoon sugar
⅛ teaspoon salt
¼ cup salted butter
½ cup cold water
Celery seed or garlic powder may be added to taste.

Grind oats in a blender. Place oats with other dry ingredients in mixing bowl. Cut in butter until consistency of coarse bread crumbs. Mix in cold water. Shape dough into a 9-inch roll. Wrap in plastic wrap and chill for at least 3 hours. Slice into ⅛-inch-thick slices and place on an ungreased, foil, or parchment-lined baking sheet. Flatten with fork tines. Bake at 375° for 12 minutes or until edges are nicely browned. Cool on racks. Serve with pumpkin, peach or apple butter. Yield: 6 dozen.

GOOD BREADS

Fetching Some Kindling

Breads listed in Mrs. J. C. Croly's 1866 book entitled *Jennie June's American Cookery Book* included cornbread, Johnny Cake, Brown Bread, biscuits, muffins, Rye and Indian, Rice Flour Bread, rusks, Hot Cross Buns, and potato rolls. Brigham Young was a fan of Buttermilk Doughnuts.

How did pioneers—in cabins where all the heat was concentrated at the hearth—get loaves to rise? In summer, Mrs. J. C. Croly put her bread pans in the sun. In winter, she advised cooks to heat two bricks to one hundred degrees or more. Set the mixing pan on the bricks, and mix and knead there. Divide the dough into tins, place on the heated bricks and "cover well with woolens." What about yeast? When she lacked baker's yeast, Croly made her own from hops.

A little House well fill'd, a little Field well till'd, and a little Wife well will'd, are Great Riches. --1735

GOOD BREADS

SHARON RYAN'S WHOLE WHEAT BREAD
--Great Smoky Mountains National Park

> 1 cup stone ground whole wheat flour
> 2 cups unbleached bread flour
> ¾ cup oats
> ¼ cup wheat germ
> 2 tablespoons softened butter
> 1½ teaspoons salt
> 2 tablespoons sorghum molasses
> 2 tablespoons dark brown sugar
> 1 packet active dry yeast
> 1¼ cups lukewarm milk (105°)
> ¾ cup raisins

In a large mixing bowl combine all ingredients to form a loose dough. Knead by hand 10 minutes or machine 5 minutes until smooth. Place in a lightly greased bowl, cover and allow to rest 1 hour. The dough will rise but may not double in bulk.

Transfer dough to a lightly oiled surface and shape into a log. Place in a greased 9x5-inch loaf pan and cover with lightly greased plastic wrap. Allow to rise in a warm place 1 to 1½ hours or until loaf has crested 1 to 2 inches over rim of pan. Bake in 350° preheated oven for 35 to 50 minutes. Great for toast or sandwiches. Yield: 1 loaf.

GOOD BREADS

Freshly stone ground meal or flour is aromatic and tastier than meal or flour from a supermarket. Cornbread baked in a cast iron skillet has a delicious crisp crust. For a moister bread, use 2 eggs.

MOM'S CORN BREAD
--The gristmill at Hart's Square

> 1½ cups stone ground corn meal
> ½ cup unbleached, all purpose or bread flour
> 1 tablespoon baking powder
> 3 tablespoons sugar
> ½ cup shortening, melted
> 1 teaspoon salt
> 1 egg, slightly beaten
> 1 cup milk

Stir dry ingredients together. Beat egg with milk and add to dry ingredients. Add shortening that has been heated to the smoking point in the skillet in which you will bake the cornbread. Mix again. Return batter to the hot pan and bake at 425° for 20 to 25 minutes. Turn onto a warm plate and serve at once. Yield: 8 servings.

APPLE JOHNNY CAKE
Add 3 peeled and sliced apples to the basic corn bread (Mom's). Baking time may need to be increased 5 minutes.

CRACKLING BREAD
Add a cup of ground or finely chopped pork rinds (cracklings) to the basic corn bread.

GOOD BREADS

Joseph Smith (1805-44), founder of the Mormon Church, enjoyed a buttermilk cornbread, which he knew as "Mormon Johnnycake." It was sweetened with 2 tablespoons of honey or molasses.

BUTTERMILK CORN BREAD

A cup of corn kernels cut from leftover corn on the cob may be added. A chopped red bell pepper may also be added for color. Dripping or drippings were flavored fats like bacon fat saved from frying.

1¼ cups yellow cornmeal
¼ cup flour
1 teaspoon baking powder
1 teaspoon salt
1¼ cups buttermilk
½ teaspoon baking soda
2 beaten eggs
2 tablespoons dripping, melted lard, corn oil, butter, shortening

Combine corn meal, flour, salt and baking powder; mix well. In a small bowl, beat buttermilk with soda until foamy. Make sure no lumps of soda remain. Combine both mixtures. Add eggs. Stir in lard. Pour into a greased hot ovenproof skillet. Bake at 450° for 20 minutes or until light brown on top and pulls away from sides. Yield: 9 servings.

GOOD BREADS

Flatbread is a thin, often unleavened cracker made in large sheets or circles. Matzo is one of the best known. Less well-known but equally delicious is the Italian *Farinata* (a chickpea flour flatbread), which is known in the Nicoise region of France as *Socca*, and in Argentina and Uruguay as *Faina*. Norwegians favor *Lefse* made with riced potatoes or flatbread made with whole wheat.

FLATBREAD
-- St. John's Lutheran Church Centennial Cookbook, 1971

> **1 cup buttermilk**
> **¼ cup butter, melted**
> **½ cup corn syrup**
> **¼ cup brown sugar**
> **1 teaspoon salt**
> **2 scant cups all purpose flour**
> **2 cups stone ground Graham flour**
> **1 teaspoon baking soda**

Mix ingredients. Chill. Take small amount of dough, roll very thin with lefse rolling pin (i.e., one with a small diameter). Transfer to cookie sheet. Cut in 3-inch rectangles. Bake at 375° for 10 minutes or until they begin to brown.

GOOD BREADS

In the Old Country, Irish Brown Bread was basically

Irish Soda Bread—using Graham flour. In the New World, Boston Brown Bread became a steamed loaf—sometimes baked in a bowl, sometimes steamed in a round tin—combining Indian cornmeal and rye flour, plus molasses and raisins for sweetness. Saturday night suppers were often Boston Baked Beans served with coleslaw and Brown Bread. When New England's pioneers lacked cornmeal, they substituted bean flour, and made a loaf called horsebread. It was not particularly tasty, but it served people with hearty appetites.

BOSTON BROWN BREAD
--Miss E. J. Thompson, 1885

One cup rye flour
two cups Indian [cornmeal]
two cups wheat flour [all purpose]
one cup Graham [whole wheat]
one pint milk
one teaspoonful soda
two teaspoonsfuls cream tartar
one-half cup molasses
a little salt

Boil in a tin [ovenproof-bowl or steamed pudding mold] for 3 hours and bake in oven one hour. Yield: one round loaf.

GOOD BREADS

Doughnuts have a long history in the Old World. They were introduced to the New World by the Dutch as oliekoecken (oil cakes, fried cakes). The Dutch prepared them for the Christmas season and for other special occasions. The Pennsylvania Dutch fried batches of fastnachts on Shrove Tuesday. Doughnuts or "dough nuts" were originally leavened with yeast, but with the invention of baking powder, they became more cakelike. Sailors on whaling ships were often rewarded for processing a large whale with doughnuts cooked in the huge try pots--in whale oil. Sitting around with full stomachs, they carved whale tooth ivory into baking tools for the little women back home.

Doughnuts were originally made without holes and were thus sometimes doughy in the center. In 1857, a round cookie/biscuit cutter was patented, with an extra (smaller) round piece that could be snapped into the center to cut holes. Doughnuts are big business today—seldom made at home. 375° is the proper fat temperature for doughnut frying.

FITZPATRICK HOUSE CRULLERS
--Lang Pioneer Village

⅓ cup butter
½ cup sugar
1 teaspoon baking soda
¼ teaspoon salt
1¾ cups flour
3 eggs, beaten
fat for frying
sugar and cinnamon

Cream together butter and sugar. Add eggs, and mix well. Then stir in baking soda, salt, flour. Heat fat in frying pan. Drop spoonfuls of batter into the pan and fry until golden on each side. While still warm, roll in a mixture of sugar and cinnamon.

GOOD BREADS

Pretzels can be salty or sweet, and arranged in knot or stick form. This chewy, addictive Austrian or German form of bread reached America about 1824.

SOFT PRETZELS

3½ cups all purpose flour
2 tablespoons light brown sugar
1 teaspoon salt
1 package active dry yeast
1 cup 120° water
1 tablespoon butter or lard
1 beaten egg yolk
1 tablespoon water
pretzel salt

Mix 1 cup flour, sugar, salt and yeast. Stir yeast and butter into warm water in a large mixing bowl. Beat 2 minutes at medium speed in mixer with dough hook. Add ½ cup flour. Beat at high speed 2 minutes. Remove bowl from mixer stand. With spoon, stir in enough additional flour to make a soft dough. Turn out on floured board. Knead 5 minutes. Place in greased bowl, turning so that a greased side faces up. Cover; let rise in warm place for 40 minutes.

Return dough to floured surface. Divide dough into 12 equal pieces. Roll each into a 20-inch rope. Shape into pretzels or simple rings. Place on greased baking sheets. Cover; let rest 5 minutes.

Mix egg yolk and 1 tablespoon water. Using a pastry brush or a nylon paint brush that you reserve just for baking, brush yolk mixture on pretzels to form glazed surface. Sprinkle with pretzel salt. Bake at 375° for 15 minutes or until golden and baked through. Cool on racks. Yield: 12 pretzels.

BEST BEANS

Succotash—corn and beans—was the most common re-past eaten by Native Americans of the Atlantic coast. Fish, fowl, raccoon, squirrel, bear or venison was sometimes added to the pot. European newcomers readily adopted the basic vegetable dish. The correct proportions, according to Catherine Beecher, are two-thirds corn and one-third beans—with the cobs boiled in the mixture for a time to add their flavor. Which sort of beans? My dear grandmother voted for "shell" beans, which we raised, ate fresh, and canned by the quart.

The cultivation of beans in the Americas dates back 8,000 years. The varieties include the pinto, the red, the lima, the turtle or black, the kidney, and various small pea or navy beans. After 1492, many of these beans were taken to Europe and cultivated. So by the time the Pilgrims arrived, they were already familiar with them. They usually chose small white pea beans for baked beans, but other cooks favor Great Northerns for their "mouth feel."

SUCCOTASH
   --Carrie Shepard manuscript, 1915 to 1929

1 cup of cooked limas
2 cups canned corn
½ teaspoon salt
½ teaspoon sugar
⅓ teaspoon black pepper
1 tablespoon butter
¾ cup cream

Combine ingredients cook in double boiler.
Yield: 6 servings.

The restaurant at the Museum of Appalachia serves pinto beans with cornbread and fried green tomatoes. There's peach cobbler for dessert. Don't call me late for dinner.

BEST BEANS

PECOS PINTOS

This is a rib-sticking dish that a chuck wagon cook might ladle out to hungry cowboys. Garlic may be added to taste. The dish may be simmered all afternoon over a campfire or in a pot hung in an open hearth.

>2 cups dry pinto beans
>¼ pound salt pork, diced
>1 cup chopped onion
>2 teaspoons salt
>freshly ground black pepper to taste
>2 cans (16 ounces each) tomatoes
>1 large bell pepper, diced
>1 tablespoon sugar
>hot sauce to taste

In a bean pot or casserole, cover beans with water; soak overnight. Do not drain. Add salt pork, onion, salt and pepper. Simmer, covered, for 2 hours. Add tomatoes, bell pepper, sugar and hot sauce. Cover and simmer another 3 hours. Serve over corn bread. Yield: 8 to 10 servings.

In 1860, widow Mary Cawker bought the Four Mile House, an inn on the site of Four Mile Historic Park near Denver, Colorado. Cawker served coffee, French fries, beans and salt meat to guests who spent the night.

BEST BEANS

The Chisholm Trail was named after frontier scout Jesse Chisholm who established a cattle trail from San Antonio, Texas, to Abilene, Kansas. The heyday of the trail was from 1867 until the end of the 1880s. Along the trail, bacon, biscuits, stew, chili and beans were popular dishes. Chili got its start in the early 1800s. Chisholm Trail cowboys called chili "spoon steak," while Texas herders called the same dish "a bowl of red." Black beans or kidney beans may be added to the following recipe. It may also be thickened with cornmeal or masa harina (corn flour). Consider fried okra as a side dish.

PEDERNALES RIVER CHILI
--Chisholm Trail Heritage Committee

    4 pounds coarsely ground beef, venison, elk or buffalo
    2 large onions, chopped
    garlic cloves to taste, minced
    1 teaspoon dried oregano or 1 tablespoon fresh
        chopped
    2 tablespoons chili powder
    1 teaspoon ground cumin
    salt
    hot sauce
    2 cups hot water or beef broth
    1½ cups canned whole tomatoes

Put meat and onion into a Dutch oven and cook, stirring, over medium heat until meat is lightly browned. Add remaining ingredients except salt and hot sauce. Bring to a boil. Reduce heat and simmer one hour. Skim off fat if you wish. Season with salt and hot sauce to taste. Serve with biscuits. Yield: 10 servings.

BEST BEANS

Different regions of the country came to favor particular bean dishes, usually based on beans grown in those regions.

CHARLESTON LIMA BEAN DINNER

> **4 cups dry lima beans**
> **½ pound salt pork**
> **2 onions, sliced**
> **½ cup tomato catsup**
> **½ cup celery, chopped**
> **1 green or red bell pepper, minced**

Soak beans overnight. In the morning, drain off soaking water. Cover with fresh water and boil for 90 minutes.

Brown the salt pork in a heavy skillet, turning frequently until the entire piece is brown. Add onions and cook until browned. Pour this mixture into the beans. Add catsup. Let simmer on the hearth for 6 or 7 hours, or in a 325° oven. One hour before serving, add celery and green pepper. Check level of liquid now and then so beans do not cook dry. Serve with ham hocks, coleslaw and cornbread. Yield: 8 servings.

Photo by Wayne Erbsen

BEST BEANS

Meat sources of protein always take more time and land to produce than vegetable sources do. Fortunately for the world's diet, when Christopher Columbus was exploring Cuba he noticed the many native varieties of bean. He was among the first to write about many of them, and brought seeds to Europe. Broad beans and kidney beans were quickly adopted by British farmers for their daily pottage. Beans contain healthy amounts of fiber as well as protein.

The first immigrants to New England had a preference for the little white pea bean, which became the iconic "Baked Bean" of the area. Indeed, they became "Boston Baked Beans" and Boston became "Beantown." French-Canadian immigrants in particular embraced the bean as a weekly staple.

BEST PORK AND BEANS
--Jennie June's American Cookery Book (1866)

Pick over a quart of small white beans, put them to soak over night. Set them to boil the next morning, throwing off the water, just before they reach boiling point. Cover with cold water again, put in a square pound of nice sweet salt pork and let both boil together till the beans are tender. When the beans are done, the water should have all become absorbed; they are then put in one pan to brown, and the pork in another, scoring the latter first, through the skin. Before serving set the pork in the centre of the beans. Serve with pickles and horseradish.

I eat my peas with honey,
I've done it all my life.
They do taste kind of funny,
But it keeps them on the knife.

VEGETABLES & GREENS

Pioneers with roots in Scotland or Ireland often stewed their vegetables and mashed them to create dishes such as Turnip Purry (a puree seasoned with ginger), Colcannon (shredded cabbage mixed with mashed potatoes, turnip and carrots) and Clapshot (equal parts mashed potatoes and mashed turnips). They brought to the New World a taste for kale, leeks and nettles. East European immigrants who settled near Strawbery Banke, New Hampshire, brought seeds of Ukrainian carrots, kale and parsnips.

In the New World, both Scots-Irish and Europeans encountered new favorites like Jerusalem artichokes and butternut squash. German immigrants began to make noodles with sweet potatoes.

Photo by Wayne Erbsen

BACON & GREENS
--a popular song during the Civil War

I have lived long enough to be rarely mistaken,
And had my full share of life's changeable scenes;
But my woes have been solaced by good greens and bacon,
My joys have been doubled by bacon and greens.
What a thrill of remembrance e'en now they awaken,
Of childhood's gay morning and youth's merry scenes;
When one day we had greens and a plateful of bacon,
And the next we had bacon and a plateful of greens.

VEGETABLES & GREENS

A HARVEST MENU served at the 1823 Conner House, Conner Prairie Living History Museum, Fishers, Indiana:

Popcorn, Pounded cheese, crackers, Queen Soup, Pork roast with winter vegetables, Chicken Fricassee, Dill Pickled Green Beans, Skillet Cranberries, Applesauce, Hearth Bread with fresh butter, Bread & Butter Pudding with Cherries.

BUTTERNUT SQUASH GRATIN
-- Turek Farms, King Ferry, New York

1 butternut squash, 2 to 3 pounds
apple cider
2 tablespoons minced onion
1 teaspoon gingerroot, grated
nutmeg, salt and pepper to taste
1 cup heavy cream
2 eggs

Peel, seed, then dice or grate squash. Put in a saucepan and cover with cider. Simmer until squash is very tender. Drain juice, reserve. Place squash in a buttered baking dish. Add onion and seasonings. Mix gently.

Beat eggs and cream. Pour over squash. Add half reserved cider. Bake at 350° until set, 45 minutes to 1 hour. Yield: 6 servings or more, depending on size of squash.

VEGETABLES & GREENS

A MESS OF GREENS

A pot or "mess" of greens could be made with turnip greens, collards, mustard greens, kale, spinach or coarsely chopped cabbage. The same method worked for green beans and fresh lima beans. Pioneers might cook these dishes for hours, but the modern consumer usually likes them crisp-tender. Dumplings or new potatoes could be added to the pot if it was to be the main dish. If using fat back, simmer for 20 minutes to remove salt.

1 pound ham hock, or 8 ounces fat back or "side meat"
4 cups water
3 to 4 pounds washed greens

Photo by Wayne Erbsen

If using ham hock, cover with water and simmer until it begins to get tender. Add greens. Cook until tender. Serve with cornbread or biscuits.

PEPPER VINEGAR

--Michelle Evans, Conner Prairie Living History Museum, Indiana

Chop a good quantity of ripe red peppers very small, then put them into a stone or earthenware jar with 2 teaspoons Kosher salt. Cover it, and let it sit for several days. Then boil it for a few minutes. Strain and bottle for use. Sprinkle over greens, beans, etc. Store in a cool place.

VEGETABLES & GREENS

A staple before freezing and canning, Leather Britches Beans are a food particularly associated with the Appalachian region. They are also called Fodder Beans or Shucky Beans. This pole-type bean (*Phageolus vulgaris*) has a tender pod that takes well to dehydration. The best heirloom varieties are Barnes Mountain Cornfield Bean, Pink Tip Greasy Bean and Tobacco Worm Bean. Seeds are available from the Sustainable Mountain Agriculture Center in Berea, Kentucky.

LEATHER BRITCHES BEANS
To prepare: Pick beans when pods are still green. Using a darning needle and twine, thread them through the middle of each pod and hang to dry several weeks.

To cook: Remove beans from string. Rinse. Cover with plenty of water. Add a ham hock or some pork neck bones. Simmer until tender.

CONNER PRAIRIE PUMPKIN SOUP
--The Story Inn, Story, Indiana

½ cup chopped onion
3 tablespoons butter
2 cups mashed, cooked pumpkin
1 teaspoon salt
1 tablespoon sugar
¼ teaspoon nutmeg
¼ teaspoon ground black pepper
3 cups chicken stock
½ cup light cream

Gently saute the onions in the butter until lightly browned. Add pumpkin and seasonings to the pot. Slowly add chicken broth and heat thoroughly, but do not boil. To serve, pour into a warmed tureen and add the cream. Just swirl the cream to make a decorative presentation. Yield: 4 to 6 first course servings.

VEGETABLES & GREENS

SCOUT POTATOES

This dish is served every March at the Milk River Wagon Train Nut and Gut Feed, in Malta, Montana. The event features rustic foods typical of early Montana pioneer tables: Rocky Mountain oysters (bull testicles), baked beans and Scout Potatoes (sliced potatoes with ham and cheese sauce).

5 large potatoes, sliced
1 large onion, grated
2 cups thin White Sauce
1 cup grated Cheddar cheese
2 cups cubed, cooked ham

Cook the potatoes and onion in boiling salted water for 5 minutes. Drain and arrange in a buttered casserole. Add the cheese to the White Sauce. Stir until cheese is melted. Add ham to sauce. Pour over potatoes. Bake at 350° for 45 minutes.

Yield: 4 servings.

VEGETABLES & GREENS

SALSIFY WITH CREAM SAUCE

Although it has gone out of style today, salsify or "oyster plant" was a favorite Shaker vegetable. It comes in both white and black-skinned varieties; the black-skinned scorzonera has a better flavor. Cook unpeeled or peel and cook in water acidulated with lemon juice.

2 cups peeled, cooked salsify
White Sauce (see below)
2 tablespoons chopped chives

White Sauce or "Cream Sauce" does not contain cream, but dishes featuring it are called "creamed," as in "Creamed Onions." It is a savory sauce served hot over seafood, vegetables, pasta, boiled ham, and so forth. One cup of sauce will "cream" 2 cups of onions, salsify, etc. Often nutmeg is grated over the top just before serving. Chopped parsley or pimientos may be added for color.

WHITE SAUCE

2 tablespoons butter
1½ to 2 tablespoons flour
1 cup whole milk
salt and pepper to taste
nutmeg

Melt butter over low heat. Blend in flour and whisk over low heat for 3 to 4 minutes. Slowly stir in milk. Whisk or stir until thickened and smooth. Season to taste with salt and pepper. Place in the top of a double boiler over simmering water to hold.

For thin White Sauce, use proportions of 1 tablespoon butter to 1 tablespoon flour and 1 cup milk.

Yield: 1 cup.

VEGETABLES & GREENS

ROSEMARY ROASTED POTATOES

These potatoes go well with roasted venison or turkey, cold cuts or even fried eggs. Leftovers can be used in hash or soup.

    1½ pounds small new potatoes, russets, Yukon Gold
        or fingerling
    3 tablespoons olive oil
    1 tablespoon chopped fresh rosemary
    1 tablespoon balsamic vinegar
    ½ teaspoon salt
    ½ teaspoon garlic powder or 6 cloves

Cover the potatoes with water, bring to a boil, and simmer for 15 minutes. Remove. Cut into quarters. This may be done the day before.

Whisk together the remaining ingredients except for garlic cloves. Add the potatoes and toss until covered. Place the potatoes in a single layer in a shallow baking pan. Bake at 425° for 20 to 25 minutes, stirring at least once. Done when the potatoes are fork-tender and golden.

Add garlic cloves during last 15 minutes to prevent their burning. Yield: 4 to 6 servings.

He that sows thorns should not go barefoot. --1741

VEGETABLES & GREENS

Photo by Wayne Erbsen

Lacking refrigeration, pioneer housewives were resourceful and found clever ways to use leftovers before they spoiled.

ROASTED POTATO SALAD

> **Rosemary Roasted Potatoes (page 100)**
> **olive oil**
> **2 tablespoons vinegar**
> **¼ cup chopped shallots or onion**
> **2 teaspoons Dijon mustard**
> **1 cup chopped basil**
> **salad greens**

Dice potatoes. Put in a salad bowl. Scrape drippings from roasted potatoes into a measuring cup. Add enough oil to make 6 tablespoons. Whisk in vinegar, shallots and mustard. Pour over potatoes. Taste. Add more salt if needed. Toss with basil. Allow to stand at room temperature for 1 hour. Serve over greens.

VEGETABLES & GREENS

Greens, both wild and cultivated, were important pioneer foods. Thistle, nettle, dock, lambs-quarters, kale, spinach, Swiss chard, wild violet leaves, mustard greens, turnip greens, and young dandelions were gathered early in the morning when just a few inches high, weeks before they formed flowers or seeds. All were cooked in essentially the same way, as in the following 1839 recipe:

POKE GREENS

"Poke tops or sprouts that put forth in the spring of the year are considered fine sallad by many people. Gather them when young and tender, pick them carefully, pour boiling water on, and let them stand an hour or two, to draw out the strong taste. Having ready a pot of boiling water in which a piece of bacon has been boiling till nearly done, put the poke in, and let it boil with the meat till it is tender. It will take but a short time to boil it sufficiently as it is not good when boiled very soft. Serve it with the meat, drain it well and have salt, pepper and vinegar to season it at table."

--*Kentucky Housewife* (1839)

The length of time greens should be cooked was a matter of continuing debate. Eliza Acton in *Modern Cookery for Private Families* (1845) recommended cooking them a long time: "Vegetables when not sufficiently cooked are known to be so exceedingly unwholesome and indigestible, that the custom of serving them 'crisp' should be altogether disregarded when health is considered of more importance than fashion," Acton wrote.

My maternal grandmother (b. 1888), however, relished a bowl of dandelion greens boiled just a few minutes, drained, and served cold with a dash of cider vinegar.

VEGETABLES & GREENS

Pioneer vegetables were usually "boiled vegetables." Raw vegetables are seldom mentioned, although Mary Randolph suggests a "delicate dish" of lettuce, pepper grass, chervil and cress, picked early in the morning and immersed in ice water until serving time. Randolph dresses her salad with a mixture of hardboiled egg yolk, oil, salt, sugar, mustard, and tarragon vinegar. The dish is garnished with young scallions, "they being the most delicate of the onion tribe."

Photo by Fernand L. Chandonnet

Always careful of his diet, Thomas Jefferson shunned meat except "as a condiment for vegetables," and cultivated 250 varieties in his kitchen garden. He particularly favored Hotspur and Marrowfat peas, artichokes, asparagus and Brown Dutch and Tennis-ball lettuce. Jefferson's salad crops at Monticello included spinach, endive, orach (goosefoot), mache (corn salad), pepper grass, sorrel, nasturtium flowers and cress.

"Management is an art that may be acquired by every woman of good sense and tolerable memory....the prosperity and happiness of a family depend greatly on the order and regularity established in it."
--Mrs. Mary Randolph, 1824

VEGETABLES & GREENS

ROASTED BEET SALAD

Roast beets while baking potatoes and get double use of your oven. Beet salad is delicious, winter or summer. Top with walnut pieces and crumbled goat cheese or blue cheese to make this a main dish.

Beets:
> **3 pounds medium beets**
> **1 tablespoon olive oil**
> **salt and pepper**

Dressing:
> **3 tablespoons cider vinegar or balsamic vinegar**
> **1 tablespoon prepared mustard**
> **1 tablespoon honey**
> **salt and pepper to taste**
> **¼ cup olive oil**

Greens:
> **10 cups (about 8 ounces) assorted greens or spinach, washed and chilled.**

Beets: Trim beet tops to half an inch, and scrub well. Rub with oil and place in a roasting pan. Roast at 425° for 1 hour or just until tender when pierced.

Remove from oven, and cool until they can be handled. Remove the tops with a knife. Slip skins from beets, using a vegetable peeler for tough spots. Cut each beet in half, and then cut each half in 4 wedges. Put wedges into a bowl and marinate for 2 hours at room temperature in a little of the dressing, stirring when you think of it.

Dressing: Whisk ingredients together, adding the oil gradually in a thin stream.

Preparing Salad: Toss chilled greens and remaining dressing in a serving bowl. Top with marinated beets. A little lemon or orange zest on top doesn't hurt. Yield: 6 servings.

VEGETABLES & GREENS

Parsnips were considered sweeter if eaten after the first frost.

BUTTERED PARSNIPS
   --Johnson manuscript, begun 1867

> parsnips
> butter
> pepper
> salt
> parsley
> cream

[Cut off tops.] Boil tender and scrape. Slice quarter inch thick lengthwise. Put into saucepan with 3 tablespoons melted butter, pepper, salt & chopped parsley. Shake over the fire till the mixture boils. Lay the parsnips in a dish & pour the sauce over them. Garnish with parsley. It improves this to stir a few spoonfuls of cream into the sauce after the parsnips are taken out, boil up and pour upon them.

The sourness of sauerkraut is mellowed with the addition of a little apple. This side dish is delicious with sausage or pork chops.

SAUERKRAUT WITH APPLE
   1 quart sauerkraut
   ½ cup sugar
   2 onions, diced
   1 tablespoon vinegar
   1 apple, peeled, cored and diced
   1 tablespoon butter or bacon fat

Cover the sauerkraut with water. Add the apple, one diced onion, sugar and vinegar. Simmer 30 to 45 minutes. Then add remaining onion which has been browned in butter or bacon fat. Serve immediately. Yield: 4 servings.

FRUITS

Photo by Wayne Erbsen

Pioneers were as fond of sweets as anyone — especially puddings. Basic puddings were simply flour stirred into water and steamed in a cloth or mold.

The term pudding comes from the Old French *boudin*, black or blood pudding. So it ranges from a meat mixture stuffed into an intestine or a stomach (like haggis) to a soft, creamy dessert thickened with cornstarch, arrowroot, cornmeal, eggs or oatmeal. It may feature fruit or milk. Early puddings used animal innards as forms, but a buttered and floured cloth had assumed that duty by the seventeenth century. Today's pudding may be stirred in a pot, steamed in a mold or baked in an oven. Hasty pudding, based on cornmeal, flour or oatmeal, is stirred up quickly for breakfast.

A Fool is stewed fruit folded into whipped cream. In Britain, the word has come to indicate any dessert. Cranachan, a Scots dish, is a fool with toasted oatmeal folded in.

> I sing the sweets I know, the charms I feel
> My morning incense and my evening meal,
> The sweets of hasty-pudding, come dear bowl,
> Glide o'er my palate, and inspire my soul.
>
> There first was heard the welcome strain
> Of axe and hammer, saw and plane.
> But Hark, I hear the Pancake-Bell
> And fritters make a gallant smell.
> --Shrove Tuesday song

FRUITS

Many pioneer puddings came from England, as revealed by their names: Marlborough, Nesselrode, Nottingham, Sunderland, and Whitpot. But cooks in North American soon altered their recipes to include local ingredients such as huckleberries and cranberries.

STEAMED CRANBERRY PUDDING

Tangy cranberries — also known as "fen berries" or "bounce berries"--grow wild in boggy areas and could be gathered by pioneer children in the fall, before frost blackened the fruit. They keep well in barrels of water in a root cellar.

1½ cups flour
½ teaspoon salt
1 teaspoon baking soda
½ teaspoon baking powder
2 cups cranberries, sorted and halved
½ cup molasses
½ cup brown sugar
grated rind of one orange (optional)
1 egg
½ cup hot water

Mix all ingredients and steam in a greased container for one and a half hours. Serve warm with Vanilla Sauce. Yield: 6 servings.

VANILLA SAUCE

½ cup butter
1 cup sugar
½ cup cream
1 tablespoon vanilla extract

Combine all ingredients in a double boiler. Boil five to eight minutes, until slightly thick. Yield: 6 servings.

FRUITS

OOTHING Rice Pudding could bake slowly while the housewife tended to another chore. The Strawbery Banke website offers this recipe:

A RICE PUDDING
--American Cookery (1798)

"One quarter of a pound of rice, a stick of cinnamon, to a quart of milk (stirred often to keep from burning) and boil quick, cool and add half a nutmeg [grated], 4 spoons rose-water, 8 eggs; butter or [line with] puff paste a dish and pour the above composition into it, and bake one and a half hour."

SWEET POTATO PUDDING

Reminiscent of Pumpkin Pie, Sweet Potato Pudding works as a hot side dish with ham, or cold for breakfast. The grated potatoes give it the texture of coconut. I sometimes mix leftover mashed butternut or Hubbard squash in with the potatoes.

> 2 eggs
> 1 cup milk
> ¼ cup melted butter
> 1½ cups raw grated sweet potatoes
> ¼ teaspoon mace
> ¼ teaspoon ginger
> ½ teaspoon ground cinnamon
> ½ cup sugar (brown or white)
> 1 teaspoon vanilla

Beat eggs. Add milk and melted butter. Mix well. Then add remaining ingredients. Put into a greased casserole and bake at 325° until set, about 1 hour. Yield: 4 servings.

FRUITS

HITMAN Mission National Historic Site has done an admirable job of collecting authentic recipes served along the Oregon Tail. Hardtack and jerky were common trail foods, but when they had time to cook, the pioneers also enjoyed this dessert, reminiscent of both Summer Pudding and French Toast.

OREGON TRAIL APPLE TREAT

4 to 5 slices buttered bread
2 cups unsweetened applesauce
2 beaten eggs
2 cups milk
½ cup sugar
½ teaspoon salt

Line the bottom of a buttered pudding dish with bread. Cover with applesauce. Repeat layers until the dish is half full, finishing with bread on top. Whisk together eggs, milk, sugar and salt. Pour over layered bread. Bake at 350° until set—about 25 minutes. Serve cold with cream, sugar and cinnamon or grated nutmeg.

Photo by Fernand L. Chandonnet

FRUITS

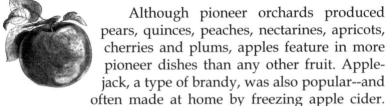

Although pioneer orchards produced pears, quinces, peaches, nectarines, apricots, cherries and plums, apples feature in more pioneer dishes than any other fruit. Applejack, a type of brandy, was also popular--and often made at home by freezing apple cider. Laird and Company of New Jersey began distilling it in 1780.

APPLE SNOW
   --Whitman Mission National Historic Site

   10 apples
   1 cup water
   grated rind of 1 lemon
   10 eggs, separated
   1 cup sugar

Peel and core apples. Simmer in water with lemon rind until tender. Force through a colander or sieve and cool.

Beat egg whites stiff and fold into apples. Add sugar, and continue beating until stiff. Serve in a glass dish with custard sauce made with the egg yolks. Good with sponge cake or lady fingers.

Photo by Wayne Erbsen

Frontier Culture Museum

FRUITS

Pioneers like the Tompkins family started orchards wherever they moved. John and Sarah Tompkins moved first from Virginia to Missouri and then in 1857 headed their wagon toward Texas. Their apples, pears and plums were well known in Parker County. The Tompkins cabin is now featured at the Log Cabin Village in Fort Worth.

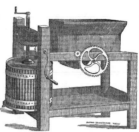

APPLE STUFFING
Adapted from *The Woman's World Fruit Book*, 1928.

Dried apples were a staple of the pioneer kitchen — used in pies, cobblers, cakes, applesauce and other dishes. This stuffing is suitable for duck, goose or pork. Chopped prunes and/or onions may be added. Vermont Common Crackers, invented in the 1820s, were crushed with a wooden mortar and pestle and used for stuffing if no bread crumbs were available.

> **4 large apples or equivalent dried apples**
> **1½ cups dry bread crumbs or cracker crumbs**
> **1 teaspoon powdered sage**
> **1 teaspoon salt**
> **¼ teaspoon paprika**
> **grated rind of 1 lemon**
> **about ⅔ cup water or stock**

Peel, core, and finely chop the apples. Blend with the crumbs and seasonings, moisten with water or stock and use to fill body of bird or cavity from which bone was taken (if shoulder of pork is being used).

A stuffed bird takes longer to cook than a bird which is not stuffed.

FRUITS

Hale Farm and Wheatfield Village in Bath, Ohio, recreates a struggling town in the Western Reserve during America's formative years. Special events include a Civil War-style Thanksgiving dinner. Thanksgiving was a brand new national holiday, declared in 1863 by Abraham Lincoln and observed in November. Long before, however, many cultures had celebrated with a similar harvest celebration.

A large bowl of applesauce often stood on the pioneer table, no matter what meal was being served. Fresh apples were used at harvest time. Dried apples were used when fresh were not available.

APPLESAUCE

Select apples that are firm and free of bruises. Apples may be refrigerated — but are best when used within one month.

Applesauce is a traditional dish with roast pork. It's also delicious with Macaroni and Cheese. In Tennessee, pioneers layered Stack Cake with applesauce.

8 medium Golden Delicious, Northern Spy,
Rhode Island Greening or Baldwin apples
2 tablespoons sugar
1 teaspoon cinnamon
pinch ground cloves or nutmeg
dash of salt

Peel, core and chop apples. Cook in saucepan with ¾ cup water over medium heat, until tender, about 20 minutes. Keep covered, but stir occasionally.

Remove from heat. Coarsely mash. Add sugar, cinnamon, and cloves. Serve warm or cold. Yield: 5 cups.

FRUITS

Settlers from the British Isles brought with them to the New World a taste for stewed fruit, especially stewed fruit mixed with cream. Sometimes the cream was added without whipping it.

GOOSEBERRY FOOL

Quick to prepare, Gooseberry Fool has been a favorite in Scotland since Elizabethan times.

3 cups (about 1 pound) ripe gooseberries,
   stems and tails removed
about ½ cup sugar
¼ cup water
1 cup heavy cream
2 tablespoons sugar
½ teaspoon vanilla

Mash prepared gooseberries. Mix with sugar and water in a saucepan. Cook over medium heat, stirring, until gooseberries are soft. Add more sugar if the mixture is too tart. Cool.

When ready to serve, whip the cream with the sugar and vanilla until soft peaks form. Fold in the fruit until you get a marbled effect.

Yield: 6 servings.

> "He clicked his tongue at the horse, took the plow handles firmly in hand, and put his weight on the plow handles and weighted the blade, and the plow moved, the earth turned, the dark earth turned and the smell of the earth came into the air and the row opened to him and yielded to him and was ready." --John Ehle, *The Land Breakers* (1964)

ICE CREAM

Even before the dasher-type ice cream freezer was invented by Nancy Johnson in Philadelphia in 1843, pioneers still managed to make ice cream.

ICE CREAM IN A CAN
>   --Dallas Heritage Village
>   **2 beaten eggs**
>   **½ cup sugar**
>   **2 tablespoons cornstarch**
>   **1 teaspoon vanilla extract**
>   **1 cup whole milk**
>   **1 cup light cream**
>   **1 cup rock salt**
>   **1 pound crushed ice**

Photo by Wayne Erbsen

Museum of Appalachia

In a medium bowl, whisk together the sugar and cornstarch. Then beat in the eggs. Next add the milk, cream and vanilla. Pour into a 12-ounce coffee can. Cover with waxed paper or plastic and then the can lid. Place the filled can into an empty 34½ ounce coffee can. Fill empty space with crushed ice, sprinkling generously with rock salt. Cover with lid. Roll around the floor for 20 minutes or until frozen.

The first published recipe for chocolate brownies appeared in the Sears and Roebuck catalogue in 1897. Previously brownies were flavored with molasses.

CAKES, PIES & COOKIES

Photo by Wayne Erbsen

Baked goods and confectionary are more technically advanced than stewing, roasting and baking in the ashes. Consequently, the closest to cake many pioneers came was Ash Cake.

Most of the sugar used by pioneers was brown, which explains why Laura Ingalls was very surprised when her mother baked heart-shaped Christmas cookies — containing both white sugar and white flour. White sugar came in the form of conical loaves — 3 to 30 pounds — wrapped in blue paper. Pieces were cut from the loaf with a "nipper," or sugar was scraped from the surface of the cone and pulverized in a mortar. Then it was sifted.

CAKE FLOUR

Put 2 tablespoons of cornstarch in the bottom of a 1-cup measuring cup. Fill with all purpose flour. Sift.

Yield: 1 cup cake flour

Commonly sweetened with molasses, gingerbread was baked both as cakes and cookies. The Conner Prairie Museum holds an annual gingerbread house competition for the cookie form. The following cake recipe came from a handwritten 1947 letter by Laura Ingalls Wilder to Sylvia Rholena. Wilder was known for her gingerbread throughout Wright County, Missouri. This type is sometimes known as "hot water gingerbread."

CAKES, PIES & COOKIES

LAURA INGALLS WILDER'S GINGERBREAD
        --from Joan Noon, site coordinator, Walnut Grove Pioneer Village, Long Grove, Iowa

1 cup light brown sugar
1 cup molasses
3 cups flour
½ cup shortening
2 eggs, well beaten
½ t. salt
1 teaspoon ginger
1 teaspoon cinnamon
1 teaspoon allspice
1 teaspoon cloves
2 teaspoons baking soda
1 cup boiling water

Cream sugar and shortening. Add molasses and mix. Put baking soda in a one cup glass liquid measuring cup. Hold cup over mixing bowl and add one cup boiling water. Let foam run over into bowl until cup is full of the water. Mix.

Sift spices and salt with flour into above mixture and mix thoroughly.

Add at the last the 2 well-beaten eggs. Fold them in lightly but well.

Pour into a greased 9" by 13" pan and bake at 350° for 30 minutes or until a toothpick comes out clean. Serves 20.

Hint: Raisins, nuts, or candied fruit maybe added if you wish. Dollops of whipped cream make a pleasant garnish.

CAKES, PIES & COOKIES

Cake was a luxury made for special occasions. The traditional pound cake sailed from England to the colonies. It contained a pound each of four main ingredients: white flour, white sugar, butter and eggs. Beaten eggs supplied all the leavening. Many old receipts tipped in a glass of brandy.

This rich, dense cake keeps well in a covered container. It also freezes well. It is so rich that it is usually not frosted, although it may be drizzled with a syrup or dusted with confectioners' sugar. It becomes especially memorable when dolloped with fresh fruit and whipped cream.

Lettice Bryan's *The Kentucky Housewife* (1847) contains a recipe for Indian Pound Cake — made with cornmeal.

Pound cake could be baked by cooks who couldn't read or lacked a cookbook for reference. When baking powder was developed at the end of the 1800s, the recipe began to rely less on the leavening power of eggs and more on baking powder. Today's recipes are somewhat lighter.

> *The savor or smell [of mint] rejoyceth the heart of man, for which cause they use to strew it in chambers and places of recreation, plesure, and repose, and where feasts and banquets are made.* --John Gerarde, 1597

CAKES, PIES & COOKIES

OLD FASHIONED POUND CAKE
--Virginia Egg Council

 In most early cake directions, eggs are separated and beaten separately. The whites were whisked to a stiff peak. Eggs take about an hour to come to room temperature, but the process can be speeded up, advises the Council, by putting the eggs (in their shells) in a bowl of clean hot water for 5 to 10 minutes.

4 sticks unsalted butter
3½ cups sugar
10 eggs
1 teaspoon mace
2 tablespoons liquid flavoring (vanilla, orange or lemon extract or a fruit-flavored liqueur)
4 cups flour

Bring all ingredients to room temperature. Grease and lightly flour a 10-inch tube pan. Preheat oven to 350°.

Cream butter and sugar until nearly white and fluffy. Beat in eggs, one at a time. Add remaining ingredients and mix well. Pour batter into pan and bake for 1½ hours or until it tests done. (If the top is becoming too dark, cover cake with foil.)

Cool, remove from pan and serve, dusted with confectioners' sugar.

An alternative is to bathe the cake with Orange Syrup while it is still warm. Pierce top of warm cake with a skewer. Then pour over Orange Syrup for added flavor and moistness.

Yield: 12 servings.

CAKES, PIES & COOKIES

ORANGE SYRUP

1¾ cups plus 2 tablespoons sugar
3½ cups water
1 cup Grand Marnier liqueur or orange juice

Bring sugar and water to a rolling boil in a saucepan, stirring to dissolve sugar. Add Grand Marnier or orange juice. If mixture does not measure five cups, add water to reach 5 cups. Store in an airtight container for 1 month to drizzle on cakes and sweet breads. Yield: 5 cups.

Now that berries are flown in year-round from places like South America, we have forgotten the delight of picking and eating fresh berries — usually available for only two or three weeks a year. Blueberry Pie is one of my absolute favorite foods. I began to cook one summer morning at age 12 — when I arrived home from our private blueberry patch with a pail of berries — and Mom didn't have time for muffins.

BERRY PIES
--Mrs. Lincoln's Boston Cook Book, 1883
Pick over the berries and sprinkle slightly with flour; add sugar to taste — about one cup for a quart of fruit. Do not spoil the fruit flavor by using spices. Bake in a deep plate, with two crusts.

> *Apple pie without cheese is like a kiss*
> *without a squeeze.*
> --Old English rhyme c. 1750

CAKES, PIES & COOKIES

In the ole-timey Appalachians, Apple Stack Cake was a showpiece of four to six layers served at weddings and on holidays. Some recipes use a very short dough that rolls out like pie crust. Some versions are a delicious yellow cake. For filling, use chunky homemade applesauce, or try the following triple-apple mix. Many fans think the cake is best when two days old—but it seldom lasts that long. The top may be covered with sifted confectioners' sugar.

"An example of a complex recipe that has remained popular in Appalachia is the stack cake, also called the dried-apple stack cake. This traditional cake is delicate, highly flavored, and low in fat.... It stores well, slices thin, and looks classy, comprising six to twelve ginger-flavored layers covered with a spicy applesauce; the sauce soaks into the cake, softening it and allowing the flavors to mingle."
    -- Mark F. Sohn, "Appalachian Food," in *The Oxford Encyclopedia of Food and Drink in America* (2004).

APPLE STACK CAKE
    --Mountain Farm Museum, Oconaluftee Visitor
    Center, Tennessee
Cake:
    ¾ **cup sugar**
    ¼ **cup softened butter**
    1 egg
    ½ **cup molasses**
    1 cup all purpose flour
    1 teaspoon baking powder
    ¾ **teaspoon baking soda**
    ¼ **teaspoon grated nutmeg**
    ¼ **teaspoon powdered allspice**
    ½ **teaspoon cinnamon**
    ½ **teaspoon salt**
    ½ **cup buttermilk or sour milk**

CAKES, PIES & COOKIES

Filling:

1 quart dried apples or 6 large fresh apples (Granny Smith, Winesap, Wealthy), peeled, cored and sliced.
water
1 cup unsweetened applesauce
1 cup apple butter
¼ cup molasses

Cake: Cream sugar and butter. Add egg and beat well. Stir in molasses. Sift dry ingredients together. Stir in egg mixture and buttermilk alternately until stiff dough is formed.

Knead on floured surface 5 minutes. Divide into 5 equal portions. Grease and flour 5 9-inch round pans. Pat dough into bottom of each. Bake at 350° for 10 minutes. Layers will be about a quarter inch thick. Remove layers and cool on racks.

Photo by Fernand L. Chandonnet

Filling: Place dried or fresh apples in pot and cover with water. Cook over medium heat until soft, 10 to 15 minutes. Drain well. Then mash apples until they are the consistency of mashed potatoes, leaving smaller pieces of apple intact. Add applesauce, apple butter and molasses. Cool.

Assembly: Place cake layer on plate. Spread with apple mixture. Repeat, ending with cake. Cover and refrigerate up to 2 days before serving.

He that waits upon Fortune, is never sure of a Dinner. --1736

CAKES, PIES & COOKIES

Based on egg whites rather than butter, glossy and delicious, White Mountain Frosting or 11-Minute Frosting was once popular, and I prefer it to butter cream. You can find those recipes anywhere, but here is an unusual frosting you may want to attempt. It produces something like Royal Icing—good for frosting petit fours or gingerbread cookies.

WHITE FROSTING
--Ellen Terry Johnson, *Hartford Election Cake*, 1889

>**egg white**
>**pulverized sugar [i.e., confectioners' sugar]**
>**rose water**
>**vanilla**
>**lemon juice**

To the white of one egg, take one and a quarter cups of pulverized sugar. Stir in the sugar without beating the egg. Add three drops rose water, ten of vanilla, and the juice of half a lemon. It will at once become very white, and will harden in a very few moments, which is its chief claim to distinction.

CAKES, PIES & COOKIES

Fans of Pumpkin Pie will relish the taste of Sweet Potato Pie. A booth at the Alaska State Fair in Palmer always sold Sweet Potato Pie. Yum, yum, yum.

SWEET POTATO PIE
    --Dallas Heritage Village

    1½ baked, mashed or riced sweet potatoes
    1 cup sugar
    ⅓ cup cream
    4 beaten eggs
    ¼ cup softened butter
    2 tablespoons flour
    ½ teaspoon salt
    1 teaspoon vanilla
    1 unbaked pie shell

Preheat oven to 450°. Mix butter with sugar, salt and vanilla. Peel potatoes before mashing or ricing. Mix with remaining items to form a smooth mixture. Pour into raw pie shell. Bake 10 minutes. Reduce heat to 325°. Bake 30 minutes more or until set. Allow to cool before serving.

Photo by Wayne Erbsen

CAKES, PIES & COOKIES

For pioneers, pie could occupy center stage at any meal. An eighteenth-century favorite was Marlborough Pudding, with a custard-like filling of applesauce, cream, lemon and sherry. Pies were baked many at a time and stored in pie safes away from pests and small children. Half a pie was considered a "piece." Sometimes half a dozen different pies were cut into six wedges. Then each pie plate was given six different flavors, and a member of the haying crew dug into each plate.

Like all pioneer foods, pies were seasonal. Sweet pies were filled with mincemeat, dried apples and raisins in the winter; rhubarb and lemons in the spring; gooseberries, blueberries, fresh currants, strawberries, cherries, green apples, and huckleberries in the summer; peaches, Damson plums, currant jelly, pumpkins, squash, sweet potatoes, and ripe apples in the fall.

Savory pies were filled with chicken, partridge, prairie chicken and venison.

EXCELLENT PIE CRUST
--*St. John's Lutheran Church Centennial Cookbook, 1971*

1 cup flour
½ teaspoon salt
1 cup lard
½ cup flour
½ cup cold water

Mix flour, salt and lard with a fork. Stir flour and water into a smooth paste. Add to first mixture. Let stand for an hour or so. Then roll out. Yield: 3 pie crusts.

CAKES, PIES & COOKIES

The kitchen at the Museum of Appalachia serves country dishes such as fried green tomatoes, Soup Beans with a muffin and fried pies. At age 85 in 2009, Faye Smiddy was still running the popular kitchen.

FAYE SMIDDY'S FRIED APPLE PIES
    --Museum of Appalachia

6 cups Granny Smith apples, cored, peeled, chopped
1 teaspoon salt
3 teaspoons ground allspice
3½ cups sugar
¾ cup water
4 cups all purpose flour
2 teaspoons baking powder
1 teaspoon salt
1½ cups shortening
½ cup milk
oil for frying

Filling: Mix apples and next four ingredients and cook on medium heat until thick. Set aside.

Dough: Cut shortening into dry ingredients until crumbly. Add milk. Roll out dough on floured surface. Use a 6-inch saucer to cut circles. Re-roll scraps for more rounds.

Assembly: Put about 2 tablespoons apple mixture in the middle of each circle of dough. Fold each circle in half. Crimp edges with fork tines. Fry in hot oil [375°] until golden.

Talents: Dig them up—bring them to the light—turn them over, polish them, and they will give light to the world.
-- The Skillful Housewife's Book, 1847

CAKES, PIES & COOKIES

 Pioneer bakers had plenty of prep work—from drying and sifting flour to pounding sugar, from shelling nuts to baking pumpkins, from pulverizing dried herbs to bringing in kindling. Children were often put to work on such tasks. With raisins close to black crepe in color, Raisin Pie was considered suitable for funeral gatherings. One food historian suggests that the time it took to seed the raisins expressed the cook's love for the deceased.

GRANDMOTHER ANDERSON'S
SOUR CREAM RAISIN PIE
--St. John's Lutheran Church Centennial Cookbook, 1971

1 cup brown sugar
1½ cups raisins, steamed
1 pint sour cream
4 eggs
1 teaspoon vanilla
¼ cup flour
½ teaspoon salt
¼ cup sugar
1 baked pie shell

Separate eggs. Put brown sugar, sour cream, flour and salt in double boiler. Cook slowly until creamy, about 15 minutes. Add egg yolks and beat until smooth. Add vanilla and raisins. Pour into baked pie shell. Whip egg whites with quarter cup sugar until stiff. Cover pie with meringue. Bake until meringue is golden.

> *One cook's a cook, two cooks are half a cook, and three cooks are no cook at all.* --Ohio, 1823

CAKES, PIES & COOKIES

AM was often spread in a baked pie shell (or tart shells) and topped with meringue or whipped cream.

Better Half's Verdict
My wife makes the best pumpkin pie I ever ate, and the best part of it is the chocolate coating on the top. White of 2 eggs beaten to a stiff froth; add pulverized sugar and grated chocolate with ½ teaspoon extract vanilla. Spread on top of the pie and let harden for a moment in the oven.
--S.E. Burch, *Country Cooking*, (1907)

Early British cookies were often called "cakes." Simmons' Shrewsbury Cake is a cookie flavored with mace. The American term "cookie" is a diminutive of the Dutch koekje, or cake. Many pioneer cookies were sweetened with molasses and contained no sugar at all. Butter or margarine could be substituted for lard.

Cookies are atypical "pioneer" foods because they require an oven, and Americans continued to cook on hearths well into the nineteen hundreds. It was a challenge to produce cookies in tin ovens, although experienced cooks performed wonders.

CAKES, PIES & COOKIES

OLD FASHIONED MOLASSES COOKIES
-- St. John's Lutheran Centennial Cookbook, 1971

These are similar to the Moravian Cookies famous around Winston-Salem, North Carolina, except that the Moravian dough is ripened in a cool place for at least three days before it is baked.

2 cups flour, sifted
½ teaspoon salt
½ teaspoon soda
¼ teaspoon ginger
1 teaspoon grated lemon rind
½ teaspoon cinnamon
½ cup lard, melted
2 tablespoons milk
½ cup dark molasses

Sift flour, salt, soda and spices. Combine melted lard, molasses, milk and lemon rind. Add dry ingredients gradually. Chill 1 hour. Roll on lightly floured board to ⅛ inch thickness. Cut out. Place on greased baking sheet. Bake at 400° about 8 minutes. Watch closely as they burn easily.

Man and melons are hard to know. --Benjamin Franklin, *Poor Richard's Almanac*, 1733

CAKES, PIES & COOKIES

Pioneers made cookies in simple shapes like diamonds and squares. With the hundreds of cookie cutters available today, the simple fluted flower has gone the way of the dodo. Sugar cookies can take any form you wish, from pumpkins to moose to the Eiffel Tower.

SUGAR COOKIES
--Lang Pioneer Village, Keene, Ontario

> 1 cup white sugar
> 1 cup softened butter
> 2 eggs, beaten
> pinch of salt
> 1 scant teaspoon baking soda
> 1 teaspoon cream of tartar
> 3½ cups all purpose flour

Cream sugar and butter. Add eggs, mixing well. Then add remaining ingredients. [Add 1 teaspoon vanilla extract, if desired.] Roll dough out on a floured surface and cut into desired shapes. Bake at 350° until lightly browned.

Photo by Wayne Erbsen

Bee Gums at Hart's Square Village

129

CAKES, PIES & COOKIES

Here comes that applesauce in yet another guise: cookies this time.

GRANDMA CODY'S APPLESAUCE COOKIES
-- Buffalo Bill Cody Homestead, LeClaire, Iowa

6 c. flour
1⅓ c. shortening
2¼ c. sugar
3 eggs
1 cup unsweetened applesauce
1 tsp. baking soda
2 tsp. baking powder

2 tsp. nutmeg
2 tsp. vanilla
1 tsp. salt

Cream shortening, sugar, eggs and vanilla. Add applesauce and mix well. Add sifted dry ingredients and blend well. Drop by heaping table-spoons on greased cookie sheet, flatten with fork dipped in sugar. Bake 10 to 12 minutes at 375°. (Do not brown.) Yield: 44 four-inch cookies.

SWEET MILK INTO SOUR
To make sweet milk into sour, put 1 tablespoon of vinegar in the bottom of a glass measuring cup. Fill with milk to amount called for. Stir. Wait 5 minutes. Buttermilk may be substituted for sour milk, or vice versa.

CAKES, PIES & COOKIES

MY friend, Mitzi, who lived for twenty years among the Amish of Pennsylvania, shared this recipe.

WHOOPIE PIES

2 cups sugar
½ cup shortening
2 eggs
Cream together.
2 tsp soda
½ cup cocoa
½ tsp. baking powder
1 cup sour milk
½ tsp. salt
1 tsp. vanilla

Mix together and add 1 cup boiling water.
Add 4 cups flour.
Mix well, drop by tablespoon on lightly greased cookie sheets.
Bake at 350° approximately 10 to 12 minutes. When cookies are cool, sandwich two cookies (flat sides facing) together with Filling. Perfect for after-school snacks.

FILLING:

2 beaten egg whites
1 tablespoon vanilla
2 cups confectioners' sugar

Blend well and add 1½ cup shortening and beat until smooth. Spread on cooled cookies.

> *What one relishes, nourishes.* --1734

CAKES, PIES & COOKIES

For a very simple berry dessert, mix fresh blueberries with vanilla yogurt. Sprinkle a few reserved berries on top. Garnish with a mint leaf. Serve at once.

With fresh berries, the following quick dessert will delight any palate.

MINTED BERRIES
3 cups blackberries or blueberries
2 tablespoons sugar
1 tablespoon finely chopped mint
2 teaspoons lemon juice

Stir together all ingredients in a bowl and let sit for half an hour at room temperature. Serve with sugar cookies. Yield: 6 servings

Photo by Wayne Erbsen

To Keep Lemons Fresh
--Catherine Owen, *Culture and Cooking*, 1881
Put them in a crock, cover them with water. They will in winter keep two or three months, and the peel be as fresh as the day they went in. Take care of course, that they do not get frosted. In summer change the water twice a week; they will keep a long time.

Better slip with foot than tongue. -- 1734

JAMS & CONDIMENTS

Pioneer housewives prided themselves on their ability to create special preserves like North Carolina's FROG Jam (figs, raspberries, orange juice and ginger). Head cheese was not the same without Mustard Pickle, nor could salt codfish be served without Milk Gravy. If there was no time to bake gingerbread for unexpected guests, the cook could reach for a jar of Brandied Peaches or fill tart shells with Strawberry Jam. Floating Island was garnished with gleaming bits of jelly. At large gatherings, some cooks assembled "seven sweets and seven sours"—a sign of the true "kitchen goddess."

For more than 30 years, Vergie Coxe cooked at the Tennessee Fall Homecomings held at the Museum of Appalachia. Vergie was known for her fried pies as well as her Apple Butter.

APPLE BUTTER

Apple Butter, Pear Butter, Pumpkin Butter—these were not simply tasty spreads for biscuits or rusks but a way to "put down" (preserve) perishable fruit. Before the advent of canning, large batches were prepared in a cast iron or copper kettle suspended over a fire in the dooryard.

10 gallons fresh cider
2 tablespoons salt
1 bushel dried apples
15 to 20 pounds of sugar
cinnamon to taste

Mix cider and salt in a cauldron. Boil cider down until there is room to add dried apples. Then start stirring. When all the apples have been added, begin adding sugar to taste. Cook until desired thickness. The mixture will darken as it cooks. Season with cinnamon to taste.

Pour into hot glass jars or "stone jars" (pottery crocks) and seal. Store in a cool place away from sunlight.

JAMS & CONDIMENTS

MUSHROOM KETCHUP

-- Beulah Bodwell manuscript, 1855

The term ketchup refers to a spicy condiment or sauce for meat or fish, deriving from the Malay kechap or fish sauce. Modern diners are most familiar with tomato catsup or ketchup, but in the 1800s these thick table sauces were created from all sorts of raw ingredients, including green walnuts, oysters, plums, cucumbers, Concord grapes and cranberries. The following recipe makes a good weekend project.

1½ pounds fresh mushrooms
1½ tablespoons pickling or other non-iodized salt
1 ounce dried boletes
3 cups hot water
2 cups white vinegar
1 small onion, peeled
1 clove garlic, peeled
10 whole allspice
4 whole cloves
3 large blades mace
2 bay leaves
½ tsp. ground ginger
½ teaspoon freshly ground pepper
¼ cup medium or dry sherry

Clean and trim mushrooms. Slice thin, and mix with the salt. Cover with a cloth, and let them stand at room temperature for 24 hours, stirring when you think of it.

The following day, combine the dried boletes with the hot tap water; let them stand an hour, covered, until soft.

JAMS & CONDIMENTS

With a slotted spoon, lift the mushrooms from their liquid — to eliminate any grit. Put the liquid through a sieve lined with cheesecloth or a clean dish towel. Put the soaked mushrooms into a blender, and puree with their strained liquid. Pour into a pot. Then puree the salted mushrooms, and add to the pot.

Puree about half a cup of the vinegar with the onion and garlic. Add this mixture to your pan with the remaining vinegar and the spices. Bring to a boil, then reduce heat and simmer for 1 to 1½ hours, or until the mixture is thick. Press the mixture through a sieve to remove the bay leaves and whole spices, then puree again, in batches, in blender or food processor.

Rinse out the pot. Return the ketchup to the pot, and bring to a boil, stirring. Stir in sherry. Remove from heat.

Ladle hot ketchup into hot, clean half-pint or pint canning jars, leaving a quarter inch of headspace. Seal according to jar manufacturer's directions. Yield: about 4 cups.

Photo by Wayne Erbsen

JAMS & CONDIMENTS

WATERMELON PRESERVES

--The Woman's World Fruit Book, 1928

Remove all rind and white portions of the melon. Seed and dice the pink pulp, weigh and add half as much sugar as melon. To each six pounds of melon, add the juice and grated rind of two lemons. Cook very slowly until quite thick. At first the preserve will have the appearance of becoming very watery, but upon further cooking it will gradually thicken. Turn into sterilized jars.

WILD CHERRY JELLY

--Helen Nicolay's recipe notebooks, 1880s-1950s

Put cherries into a pot with their stems as they are picked (in bunches). Do not wash them. Stew down until there is no more juice to extract. Then strain through a [jelly] bag. Weigh juice and add same weight of sugar. Before adding the sugar dry it in the oven, and heat the juice. Let them cook together until the mass is ready to "jell." Pour in glasses & cover when cold.

The following recipe is not a preserve, but a little extra. At the Sauer-Beckmann Living History Farm in Texas, Easter means eggs dyed with natural material and baskets woven of grass.

DYED EASTER EGGS

1 red cabbage
brown outer skins saved from a dozen yellow onions
spinach
vinegar

For purple eggs, chop the red cabbage and boil with water for 10 minutes. Add 3 tablespoons vinegar. Dye eggs.

For golden eggs, boil the onion skins with water. Add 3 tablespoons vinegar. Add hard boiled eggs. Turning them in the hot dye will result in a mottled surface. For green eggs, infuse spinach.

JAMS & CONDIMENTS

"Chow" is pidgin Chinese for food or mealtime. Chow-chow was originally a Chinese preserve of fruits, peels and ginger, probably related to Chutney. In New World households, it became an extremely popular pickle relish. There are variants on the following recipe that substitute chopped cabbage and corn kernels for the cucumbers, tomatoes and cauliflower. In other words, it's a "raid the garden, frost is coming" recipe.

CHOW CHOW
--Carrie Shepard manuscript, 1915-1929

2 cups flour
12 tablespoons powdered mustard
5 dessert spoons turmeric
vinegar
¾ cup brown sugar
2 quarts boiling/button onions
2 quarts small cucumbers sliced
6 large cucumbers
6 green tomatoes sliced
a small cauliflower, diced bit-size
3 green peppers cut fine
3 red peppers cut fine
3 cups (Kosher) salt

Mix the flour with the mustard and turmeric. Add enough vinegar to make a smooth paste. Add brown sugar. Mix. Then add more vinegar to make a gallon. Boil until thick and smooth. Set aside overnight.

Combine the Kosher salt with a gallon of water. Let the vegetables stand in this mixture overnight. Bring mixture to boiling. Then drain thoroughly, discarding brine. Add vegetables to prepared mustard mixture. Heat through. Can in pint jars. Seal. Process. Yield: 6 to 8 pints.

BEVERAGES

In addition to fresh milk and spring water, beverages consumed by pioneers included lemonade, eggnog (usually at Christmas), beer, root beer, ginger beer, Switchell, Ratafia, Raspberry Shrub, rum punch, Dandelion Wine and Milk Punch. Steaming Hot Cider, Mulled Cider and Apple Toddy were popular during winter months. Hot Chocolate was sometimes spiced with anise, cinnamon, nutmeg and/or ginger. Scuppernong Wine featuring local grapes was popular from Virginia to Ohio. Oddities include Egg Lemonade and Strawberry Water.

After the Boston Tea Party of 1773, pioneers often shunned imported tea for tisanes made from local ingredients such as dried rose hips, chamomile or blueberry leaves.

Far from general stores, pioneers sometimes reserved coffee for Sundays, consuming a brew of parched rye berries the rest of the week. During the Civil War, Union soldiers received an annual allotment of 36 pounds of coffee beans, and coffee became a regular ritual. Meanwhile, their Confederate counterparts resorted to roasting acorns, dandelion roots, peanuts, wheat and chicory.

A 1705 manuscript cookbook by D. Petre in the collection of the University of Pennsylvania Library contains recipes for raisin wine, mead, cowslip wine, and ale flavored with juniper berries. Microbreweries around the country are bringing back some of the old brews, such as spruce tip beer and (non-alcoholic) birch beer. Samuel Adams Boston Ale is considered the closest to the beer drunk during the 18th century.

It's poor pie that doesn't grease its own tin.

BEVERAGES

APPLE TODDY

--Dishes and Beverages of the Old South (1913)

Wash and core, but do not peel, six large, fair apples, bake, covered, until tender through and through, put into an earthen bowl [punch bowl] and strew with cloves, mace, and bruised ginger [gingerroot], also six lumps of Domino sugar for each apple. Pour over a quart of full-boiling water, let stand covered fifteen minutes in a warm place. Then add a quart of mellow whiskey, leave standing ten minutes longer, and keep warm. Serve in big deep goblets, putting an apple or half of one in the bottom of each. Grate nutmeg on top just at the minute of serving.

Mary Randolph's *The Virginia House-wife* lists ratafias flavored with currants, rose leaves (i.e., petals), ginger and honey. Ratafias are infusions, or domestic liqueurs, used as restoratives — prescribed for everything from boredom to rheumatism. Eleanor Parkinson's *The Complete Confectioner* (1864) recommends infusions of cherries, orange flowers, green walnuts, clove pinks and angelica root. Basil, mint, anise, cucumber peel and citrus rinds are favored by some cooks. In the colonies, ices flavored with Maraschino liqueur were called "ratafias."

Photo by Wayne Erbsen

Museum of Appalachia

BEVERAGES

A flavored wine makes a splendid treat to serve guests who enjoy trying unusual tipples.

RATAFIA

> **1 to 2 cups of cut-up fruit, vegetables,**
> **lemon peel and/or herbs**
> **¼ cup sugar**
> **¼ cup unflavored vodka**
> **1 inch vanilla bean, split lengthwise**
> **1 bottle (750 liters) of wine**

Mix the ingredients, lightly crushing the fruits, vegetables and/or herbs and dissolving the sugar. Steep in a clean glass container. Seal securely. Store in the refrigerator or root cellar for 3 to 4 weeks, occasionally shaking or stirring.

Drape clean cheesecloth in several layers in a fine sieve, and filter the liqueur. Decant into a clean bottle. Seal. Keep away from light and heat.

Photo by Wayne Erbsen

BEVERAGES

Punch, both hot and cold, was beloved of pioneers. Martha Washington served rum punch to statesmen including Benjamin Franklin and the Marquis de Lafayette. In summer months, Mount Vernon's punch would have been cooled with ice from the ice house.

MARTHA WASHINGTON'S RUM PUNCH
--Drink Boston

½ cup lemon juice
½ cup orange juice
½ cup simple syrup
3 lemons quartered
1 orange quartered
½ teaspoon grated nutmeg
3 cinnamon sticks broken
6 cloves
1½ cups boiling water

The day before: Mash the lemons, orange, nutmeg, cinnamon sticks and cloves. Add syrup, lemon and orange juice. Pour the boiling water over the mixture. Allow to cool. Strain out solids. Heat the mixture to a boil and then simmer 10 minutes. Cool. Refrigerate overnight.

Light rum
Dark rum
Orange Curacao

When ready to serve: In a punch bowl combine 3 parts juice mixture, 1 part light rum, 1 part dark rum, and ½ part orange curacao. Serve over ice. Sprinkle each cup with grated nutmeg and cinnamon.

BEVERAGES

Lemonade was a popular summer tipple for teetotalers. It is regularly on the menu at the Keene Hotel at Lang Pioneer Village in Ontario, Canada.

EGG LEMONADE

Country Cooking (Kansas, 1907) includes two recipes for Egg Lemonade. This combines the two.

juice of ½ lemon
10 ounces of water
sugar to sweeten to taste
1 "strictly fresh" egg, beaten

Make lemonade with the lemon juice, water and sugar. Pour into a clean, cold Mason jar. Add egg, and give a dash of nutmeg or ground cloves. Add ice. Shake until the egg is fully incorporated.

RASPBERRY SHRUB

Raspberry Shrub begins by preserving fresh berries as Raspberry Vinegar. In Texas, pioneers called this drink Raspberry Quencher.

2 cups fresh raspberries
vinegar
sugar

Put the berries in a glass or pottery container. Cover with vinegar. Let stand 24 hours. Pour into a saucepan, and bring to a boil. Press out all the juice through a jelly bag. Measure the juice, and add an equal amount of sugar. Simmer 20 minutes. Bottle and cork tightly. For shrub: Mix two tablespoons of vinegar in a glass of ice water.

BEVERAGES

THROUGHOUT the eighteenth and nineteenth centuries, syllabubs were favorite desserts in great households. Marion Harland's *Common Sense in the Household* (New York, 1871) recommends that sugar, wine and nutmeg be placed in a large bowl just before milking time. Then, she directs, "Let [the bowl] be taken to the cow, and have about three pints milked into it, stirring it occasionally with a spoon. Let it be eaten before the froth subsides."

In a second method, the mixture is poured into wine goblets, where it separates into a creamy top layer and a clear bottom layer. Such syllabubs were not eaten immediately but aged up to ten days before serving, and consumed with a spoon. They are served today at the King's Arms Tavern in Colonial Williamsburg.

TO MAKE SOLID SYLLABUBS

One pint of cream, half a pint of wine [such as sherry], the juice and grated peel of one lemon, sweetened to your taste; put it in a wide-mouthed bottle, shake it for ten minutes, then pour into your [wine] glasses. It must be made the evening before it is to be used.

--Sarah Rutledge, *The Carolina Housewife* (1874)

HERBS & REMEDIES

A castle's housekeeper might carry on her waist the keys to a still room. Here she would distill restoratives, roll pills and pulverize roots and herbs for special tisanes. The pioneer housewife did not own distilling equipment, but created similar medicinal liquids by infusion of local plants, barks and roots. There were remedies for quelling hysteria or giddiness, treating pain, staunching wounds, relaxing cramps, curing consumption, soothing colic and dispelling insomnia.

Readers interested in gathering wild edible plants should consult Euell Gibbons' classic *Stalking the Healthful Herbs*.

Pioneers grew herbs for both medicinal and culinary use. Chamomile, sage, parsley, bergamot, lavender, rosemary, angelica, pot marigold, rose geranium, catnip, peppermint, fennel, thyme, dill, tansy, coriander and comfrey were grown near the house. Amelia Simmons recommends thyme for soup and stuffings, sweet marjoram with turkey, parsley in soups and as a garnish for roast beef, and summer savory with sausages and salted beef. She added coriander to her Christmas Cookies. Simmons distilled her own Rose Water and used it to season Apple Pie. Sarah Hale, editor of *Godey's Lady's Book*, made her own herbal blends.

FINE HERBS FOR SOUPS AND SAUCES

Take dried parsley two ounces; of lemon-thyme, summer-savory, sweet majoram and basil, one ounce each; dried lemon-peel one ounce; these must be dried thoroughly, pounded fine, the powder mixed, sifted, and bottled.

--Sarah Hale, *The Good Housekeeper, or The Way To Live Well, and To Be Well While We Live,* 1841

HERBS & REMEDIES

Some pioneer remedies make very little scientific sense. Most of us would hesitate to apply a spider web to a wound, salt pork to a punctured heel or serve hot chocolate for insomnia and asthma as physician Benjamin Rush did in Philadelphia in the 1770s. The following "remedies" should be considered with a grain of salt.

Many pioneers adopted Native American remedies such as curing poison ivy and preventing athlete's food with jewelweed (*Impatiens capensis*). Theron Pond of New York learned about witch hazel from an Oneida medicine man. Pond discovered that an extract of the shrub was used for burns, boils and wounds. Pond made his fortune by marketing the extract commercially in 1848.

WITCH HAZEL EXTRACT

> **5 dormant winter branches**
> **1 cup distilled water**
> **1 cup grain alcohol**

Scrape the bark off the branches. Soak it in a solution of the water and alcohol for two weeks, shaking or stirring daily. Then strain, bottle, and keep in a cool place. To use, dilute with at least two parts distilled water. Use to relieve the itching and oozing of poison ivy or as a facial astringent. Dab on insect bites to relieve itching. The Mohegans used a decoction of the leaves and bark to treat bruises and cuts.

Yield: at least 6 cups (when diluted).

HERBS & REMEDIES

To demonstrate traditional uses, the Greater Fort Worth Herb Society maintains the herb garden at Pioneer Log Cabin Village, providing a glimpse of early North Texas life. "The garden contains a mix of native Texas plants and herbs used by early settlers for medicinal or culinary purposes. In the beginning, we grew strictly pioneer herbs from the 1840-1890; but through the years volunteers have added more modern herbs and more natives because of our hot summers," says the Society's Virginia McCollom.

Culinary Herbs: Basil, Bee Balm, Calendula, Chives, Dill, Lemon Balm, Mint, Oregano, Parsley, Rosemary, Roses, Sage, Turks cap (the fruit tastes like watermelon or apples and was made into jelly or syrup), Thyme and Violets.

Household Herbs: Lavender (for scenting linens in chests), Mullein (made into cough syrup), Rue and Southernwood (insect repellent), Soapwort (soap), Tansy (flavoring for beef, pancakes, salads, and cakes.)

Medicinal Herbs: Bee Balm (nausea), Catnip (headache), Echinacea (colds), Feverfew (headaches), Horehound (coughs), Lamb's Ear (anticoagulant, bandages), Rudbeckia (tape worms).

Fragrance and Visual Delight: Roses, Daylilies, Hollyhocks, Larkspur, Pansy, Johnny-Jump-ups, Violas, Chrysanthemum, Sunflower.

Gardens at Colonial Williamsburg, Strawbery Banke and adjacent to the Hugh Mercer Apothecary Shop in Fredericksburg, Virginia, also propagate herbs for culinary, household and medicinal uses.

HERBS & REMEDIES

With no physicians close by, pioneer housewives had no choice but to doctor their families, dispensing cough syrups, stitching up wounds and splinting broken limbs. Mormon housewives used wild edibles whenever they could. A Mormon remedy for fever was a tea made by infusing wild ginger roots in boiling water. Early cookbooks generally provided an appendix of remedies. *The Cook Not Mad*, for example, published in New York State in 1830, included "directions for preparing comforts for the Sick Room." It was believed that persons who were ill needed a special diet focusing on clear broths like beef tea.

Certainly some of these remedies and sickroom foods were not healing. However, one cannot discount the positive effect of loving care and the laying on of hands.

Invalids were dosed with currant jelly, rice, sago pudding, tapioca, wine jelly and sassafras jelly. Sassafras root and bark were fermented to make root beer or sassafras mead.

BEEF TEA
   --Dr. Webster, *Hartford Election Cake*, 1889

round steak
water

Chop fine one pound of round steak, carefully removing all fat. Put into a saucepan with a pint of cold water. Let it simmer on the hearth or on the back of the stove for two hours. Remove then to a hot place, and boil quickly for half an hour. Season with salt. Remove meat before serving.

FOR THE TOOTH-ACHE
   --*The Good Housekeeper*, Sarah Joseph Hale, 1841
   "If caused by a cold, a ginger poultice is the best remedy. Wet a thick flannel cloth in scalding vinegar, sprinkle it thickly over with ground ginger, and bind on the face when going to bed."

HERBS & REMEDIES

My grandmother, Ethel Kimball Bodwell Fox (1888-1979), penned these remedies on a blank page in her 1883 book, *Mrs. Lincoln's Boston Cook Book.*

COUGH MEDICINE
½ cup sugar, 2 tablespoonsfuls glycerine, juice 1 lemon.

INFLAMED VEINS
1 cup vinegar, 2 cups hot water, 2 tablespoonful salt. Wrap in flannel.

Pioneers also gathered wild plants like ginseng, young blackberry leaves, and wintergreen berries and weeds like boneset (*Eupatorium perfoliatum*). Also called thoroughwort, feverwort, and sweating plant, boneset was steeped with mint and sage and drunk to reduce fever. To promote sleep, they combined spearmint leaves, chamomile flowers, peppermint leaves and orange peel.

Many herbs are steeped or infused — but never boiled. Proportions are 1 tablespoon of dried leaves to 1 cup boiled water. Time of infusing ranges from 15 to 60 minutes.

Strawberry leaves and violet leaves: Steep for a refreshing tea.

Pennyroyal: Rub on the skin as a protection against biting insects. Another repellent: mix three parts lavender oil or eucalyptus oil to one part pure alcohol. Apply to pressure points before going outdoors.

Catnip: Steep, sweeten with honey and use as a cough syrup.

HERBS & REMEDIES

Peppermint: The oils in peppermint help to calm the digestive system and relieve pain. Drink this tea with or after meals. Simply crush fresh peppermint leaves and steep in hot water. In *The Good Housekeeper* (1839), Sarah Josepha Hale states that mint is "useful in allaying nausea and vomiting."

Chamomile: Drink a cup of this tisane once an hour for stomach distress.

Horseradish: The grated fresh root was considered a preventive for food poisoning, scurvy, tuberculosis and colic.

Honey: Honey is an antibacterial and anti-inflammatory agent. Spread on minor burns.

Salt: Reduce the swelling of a sore throat by gargling with hot salt water.

Slippery elm bark: Use as an expectorant, in cough syrups and cough lozenges.

Salt pork: When someone steps on a nail, bind the sole with a rind of salt pork. If the foot swells, bathe it in a tisane of wormwood, then bind on another rind of pork. (Sarah Hale, 1839).

Blackberries, unsweetened applesauce, rice, mashed carrots: Consume for their anti-laxative effect.

Rhubarb, prunes, figs and melons: Consume for their laxative effect.

HERBS & REMEDIES

ANKLES (WEAK)

> --Mai Thomas, *Grannie's Remedies*

Take a raw oyster in the palm of right hand, and massage the ankles with it until the oyster is almost rubbed away Do this every evening at bedtime, and the ankles will become stronger.

ANKLES (SPRAINED)

Take some caraway seeds, pound, and place into a tin basin with a little water Put on the stove and stir till the mixture thickens, then bind on the ankle. It will ease pain and inflammation.

COUGHS

Make a hole through a lemon, and fill it with honey. Roast it and catch the juice. Take a teaspoonful frequently.

HERBS & REMEDIES

Herbs were valuable around the house, too. Rosemary was sewn into cloth bags and hung in closets or put into clothes chests to discourage moths. Another anti-moth mixture is southernwood, wormwood and lavender. Vetiver root and crushed bay leaves are said to repel all sorts of insects.

Pioneers infused scented vinegars not for salad but to refresh the atmosphere. Placed in bowls, they de-scent a sick room.

ROSEMARY-MINT

12 ounces white vinegar
1 orange
2 sprigs fresh or 2 tablespoons dried rosemary
2 sprigs or 2 tablespoons dried peppermint
2 cinnamon sticks

Heat the vinegar to just boiling. Pour over the peel of the orange the rosemary, peppermint and cinnamon sticks. Let stand a week or two, capped, in a sunny spot, shaking occasionally. Pour into a fresh bottle to give as a gift.

CEDAR-SPICE

12 ounces white vinegar
1 tablespoon sandalwood chips
1 teaspoon powdered cedarwood
   or 1 tablespoon cedar chips
1 cinnamon stick
1 tablespoon whole cloves

Heat vinegar. Add remaining ingredients. Allow 1 to 2 weeks of standing in the sun.

HERBS & REMEDIES

The Carolina Rice Cook Book (1901) concludes with a section titled "Invalid Diet." Recipes came from various sources, such as this one from Maryland--a variant on Rice Pudding made with water rather than milk. Raisins may be added.

RICE JELLY
A quarter of a pound of rice, picked and washed; half

 a pound of loaf sugar, and enough water to cover it. Boil until it becomes a glutinous mass. Strain and season it with what you fancy [such as almond extract or cinnamon] and let it get cold.

TO TEST FOR HOT FAT
When the fat begins to smoke, put in a bit of bread; if it browns quickly, or while you can count sixty as the clock ticks, it is hot enough for fried potatoes, doughnuts, etc. When hot enough to brown the bread while you count forty, it will do for fish balls, croquettes, etc.
--*Mrs. Lincoln's Boston Cook Book*, 1883

PIONEER HEALTH & DIGESTION
- Eat few suppers and you'll need few medicines.
- You should not touch your eye but with your elbow.
- We drink to one another's health and spoil our own.
- You dig your grave with your teeth.
- Unquiet meals make ill digestions.

PIONEER VILLAGES

North America boasts hundreds of picturesque pioneer villages or "heritage parks" — most worthy of a day trip or an overnight visit. Some are open year-round, some only a day a year. Many offer eateries serving period food or the opportunity to hold special events such as family reunions or weddings on the grounds.

Most are not authentic places of residence, but representations or reconstructions typical of a particular era. Many consist of historic buildings moved from the surrounding countryside, stabilized, preserved, and furnished with period items.

To be independent, a village needed basic services provided by businesses like a grist mill, a saw mill, a cooperage (barrel shop) or pottery, a smithy and a general store. Larger settlements encompassed wheelwrights, schools and physicians.

If you enjoy these sites, you might also want to drive along part of the Wilderness Road Trail. This Heritage Migration Route traces the journey of 300,000 settlers who followed Daniel Boone through the Cumberland Gap. For more information, consult the Internet site www.wildernessroadva.org

> *There was never a persimmon except there was a possum to eat it.* --North Carolina proverb

This is a list of a few typical villages.

Cades Cove, Tennessee, was a favorite hunting ground for the Cherokees. It eventually drew frontiersmen and settlers from Virginia, North Carolina and upper Tennessee with its abundant game. Today it is part of The Great Smoky Mountain National Park, located near Gatlinburg and Pigeon Forge. This open-air museum contains original pioneer homesteads, barns, pastures and farmland. An 11-mile loop follows many of the turns of the original wagon roads, passing deer and wild turkey, a sorghum mill, a cable mill, and rustic log dwellings.

PIONEER VILLAGES

Caesar's Creek Pioneer Village, Waynesville, Ohio. This village can be walked through any time during daylight hours, but the cabins are open only during weekends. Structures include the Daniel Collett House (1814), the Harkrader Barn (1803), the Toll House, the 1825 Hawkin House, and the Bullskin Inn. Some cabins were lived in continuously for nearly 200 years. Special events include an old time music festival, a Civil War encampment, and a harvest festival.

Colonial Williamsburg, Virginia. Walk the streets trod by George Washington, Thomas Jefferson and Patrick Henry. Visitors experience eighteenth-century America by seeing tradesmen at work, visiting Great Hopes Plantation, touring the Governor's Palace and dining at establishments such as R. Charlton's Coffeehouse. 88 original structures with their "dependencies" (gardens and outbuildings) are spread over 301 acres, inhabited by rare breeds such as the five-toed Dorking chicken, Leicester Longwood sheep, Cream Draft horses, Milking Red Devons, Milking Shorthorns and impressive Randall Oxen.

Photo by Fernand L. Chandonnet

Governor's Palace Kitchen, Williamsburg

Conner Prairie Museum, Fishers, Indiana. This interactive living history park offers five distinct historic areas and a museum on 1,400 acres. Programs include classes for Prairie Tykes five and up.

Crab Orchard Museum & Pioneer Village, Tazewell, Virginia. This site interprets the cultural heritage of the middle Appalachian mountain region with 15 original structures dating back to 1802.

PIONEER VILLAGES

Daniel Boone Homestead, Birdsboro, Pennsylvania. Tour the Boone house and six other restored 18-century structures including a smokehouse and barn. View the original Boone spring cellar. Grounds (with lake and picnic area) open daily. Museum and buildings: Sundays noon to 4:30 p.m.

Fort Gibson, Oklahoma. The fort was garrisoned during the Indian Wars of the late 19th century. The soldiers baked bread in a large masonry oven which is fired up on Public Bake Day in March.

Frontier Culture Museum, Staunton, Virginia. Living history of pre-immigration Europe & pre-Civil War Shenandoah Valley. Seven seventeenth, eighteenth and nineteenth-century farms were transported board by brick from Europe (Germany, Northern Ireland and England), West Africa and America for exhibit here.

Gonzales Pioneer Village, Gonzales, Texas. This village includes nine structures ranging from the 1840s to the 1890s. An opry stage, a wheelwright shop, a saloon, a broom shop, a grist mill and a general store can be explored.

Har-Ben Village, Oklahoma. This assemblage constitutes the largest collection of log cabins in the Midwest. Structures include a church build of hand-made bricks, a dentist's office, a doctor's office, and a school house. Special attractions include a doll collection, a wagon collection, and an antique hearse.

PIONEER VILLAGES

Harold Warp Pioneer Village, Minden, Nebraska. This village consists of 28 buildings on 20 acres, showcasing a large private collection of 50,000 items of Americana. It includes a sod house, a prairie church, a land office, a cobbler's shop, a Pony Express office, the Elm Creek Fort (1869), 100 antique tractors and a steam carousel.

Hart's Square, Vale, North Carolina. This private village represents North Carolina in the 1840s. Its 90 structures include a tavern, a printer's office, wood sheds, a grist mill powered by a water wheel, an outdoor baking oven, a moonshine still, a Cherokee settlement, a mule-powered cotton gin, two chapels, a ground hog kiln, and a one-room schoolhouse. Open one Saturday in October.

Historic Brattonsville, North Carolina. This 775-acre living history village opens a door into plantation life in the South during the late eighteenth and early nineteenth centuries. The Bratton family founded the settlement around 1766. Today the site includes 29 structures, all open to the public. The Heritage Breed Farm preserves rare animals like the Cotswold sheep.

Historic Deerfield is a western Massachusetts open-air museum presented as a 300-year-old village. Knowledgeable guides and historic collections make visits memorable.

Jamestown Settlement, Virginia. A colony of just over a hundred men and boys founded in 1607 is considered the first successful English settlement on the North American mainland. This living history museum recreates seventeenth-century culture; it is staffed by costumed docents. Visitors may board replicas of the three ships that sailed from Britain, and visit life-size replicas of the colonists' fort and a Powhatan village. Open daily from 9 a.m. to 5 p.m. A nearby visitors' center features an introductory film and musket firing demonstrations.

PIONEER VILLAGES

Little Log House Pioneer Village, Hastings, Minnesota. Open three days a year, this reconstruction displays 45 buildings on 180 acres. The structures include a butcher shop, a post office, a church and a millinery shop. Antique car rides are available.

McMinn County Living Heritage Museum, Athens, Tennessee. Illustrates life from Cherokee prehistory through early pioneer era. The museum contains more than 2,000 historic objects including those typical of a general store.

Museum of Appalachia, Clinton, Tennessee. Established in the 1960s, this living history museum is known for folk art, country music performances, and theme days such as Fall Homecoming. The Museum, affiliated with the Smithsonian Institution, hosts more than 100,000 guests a year. Thirty buildings on 26 acres include jail cells and a cantilevered barn, as well as a house believed to have been owned by Mark Twain's parents.

Old Salem Museums & Gardens, Winston-Salem, North Carolina. Recreates the town of Salem from 1766-1840, giving visitors a chance to stroll about the early South. Structures include a Moravian church, the Winkler Bakery (home of the Moravian cookie), Salem Academy & College (America's oldest private girls' school) and a toy museum. Eleven gardens.

Old Sturbridge Village, Sturbridge, Massachusetts., is New England's largest pioneer village, covering 200 acres. Since its 1946 debut, it has been a favorite destination for school children. With over 40 structures, it recreates rural New England life from the 1790s to the 1830s, complete with stage coach rides. The structures include a Friends' Meetinghouse, a horse-powered cider mill, a law office and a parsonage. Activities include Families Cook in December. Maria Child's *The American Frugal Housewife* guides the interpretation of domestic life here.

PIONEER VILLAGES

Rural Life Museum, Burden Plantation, Baton Rouge, Louisiana. Illustrates workings of large sugar and cotton plantations. Forty acres showcase 27 structures, including a re-created nineteenth-century plantation house flanked by slave dwellings and an overseer's cottage. Tour a "sick house," commissary, sugar house and grist mill.

Rutherford County Farm Museum, Forest City, North Carolina. Antique farm and home equipment, with large murals depicting the cultivation of cotton and early textile mills.

Sabbathday Lake Shaker Village, New Gloucester, Maine. This village, founded in 1783, is the world's only remaining active Shaker community. An impressive site with 18 buildings on 1800 acres. Six buildings are open to the public during the summer.

Shaker Village of Pleasant Hill, Harrodsburg, Kentucky. With a 3,000-acre site (a National Historic Landmark), this is America's largest restored Shaker community. The Shakers were known for their streamlined furniture and dwellings, for their herb gardens and for inventing useful items like the seed packet. Tour a carpenter's shop and a craft store. Seasonal attractions include riverboat rides, rug hooking workshops and the Blessing of the Hounds (November).

Strawbery Banke, Portsmouth, New Hampshire. This popular outdoor museum began as an effort to preserve Puddle Dock, a seacoast district in Portsmouth. The 10-acre site features four centuries of history through 42 buildings, the earliest of which dates to 1695. Many of the buildings rest on their original foundations. Open daily from May 1 to October 31, 10 a.m. to 5 p.m. Culinary history interpreters cook period dishes daily. In December, marvel at a candlelight tour.

PIONEER VILLAGES

Vermillionville, Lafayette, Louisiana. This living history museum covers Acadian or "Cajun" life from 1765 to 1890. Located on the banks of Bayou Vermillion, the museum is a village of 18 structures, including six restored houses, a trapper's cabin and a school (where children were not allowed to speak French). Costumed interpreters prepare food, play music and perform Cajun dances.

Walnut Walnut Grove Pioneer Village, Long Grove, Iowa. This village reconstructs a typical crossroads settlement and stage coach stop of the 1860s. It contains 18 buildings including a bank, an 1870 train depot with caboose, the Bison Saloon and the Keppy-Nagle General Store. Open April to October.

Photo by Wayne Erbsen

Plow deep while sluggards sleep, and you will have corn to sell and to keep. --1659

159

SOURCES: GOODS & FOODS

Amish foods: Pennsylvania Dutch Birch Beer, dried beef, Shoo Fly Pies, chicken pies, spices. Amish Country Products, 7521 Richmond Road, Williamsburg, VA. (800) 786-0407.

Bison meat, bison jerky: www.buffalogal.com, www.buffalomeatusa.com, www.highplainsbison.com. Or Jackson Hole Buffalo Meat Co., (877) 283-2969.

Candied angelica, gingerbread biskits, almond comfits, blade mace, etc.: Deborah Peterson's Pantry, Harleyville, PA 19438.

Cast iron cookware, including Dutch ovens and griddles: www.castironcookware.com

Chocolate drink mix: the Historic Division of Mars, Inc. Prepared in cooperation with the Colonial Chocolate Society, the Colonial Williamsburg Foundation and Fort Ticonderoga. Finely Grated Chocolate Drink in a 12.7-ounce muslin bag. www.americanheritagechocolate.com

Dipping gourds: The Gourd Guy, Michael P. Eldredge, (704) 865-6479; michael.eldredge@yahoo.com

Fabrics, period toys, games, books: Clara Barton Birthplace Museum, P. O. Box 356, North Oxford, Massachusetts 01537. clarabartonbirthplace@bartoncenter.org

Fireplace cranes: www.rumford.com/store

Meats cut to order: Wholesome Foods Country Deli & Butcher Shoppe, Route 686 off Route 675, west of Edinburg, VA. (540) 984-8210, ext. 1.

Smokehouse ham suitable for biscuits: Benton's Smoky Mountain Country Hams, Madisonville, Tennessee. www.bentonshams.com

SOURCES: GOODS & FOODS

Soft pretzels: Dutch Country Soft Pretzels, 2758-1 Division Highway, New Holland, PA 17557.

Food products of Virginia: go to www.shopvafinest.com for peanuts, hams, summer sausage, wine, cheese, jellies, bread dipping spices, and other Virginia-grown edibles and drinkables.

Food of the Smokies: cornmeal, stone ground wheat flour, sorghum molasses, apple butter, pumpkin butter, Hot Chow Chow, pickled beets, pickled peaches, and other comestibles. (888) 898-9102 or www.thegreatsmokymountains.org

Rose water, herbal teas, mint water, pumpkin pie spice, herbs: Sabbathday Lake Shaker Village, New Glouster, Maine. (207) 926-4597.

Salt-glazed pottery, baskets, kitchen equipment: Williamsburg Pottery, Rt. 60 West, Lightfoot, VA. www.williamsburgpottery.com

Seeds of salsify, rue, Red Russian Kale, Magnus Lovage, etc.: Seed Savers Exchange, Decorah, Iowa. (563) 382-5990.

Seeds of Melon Banana, African horned cucumber, rutabaga, Brazilian orange eggplant, etc.: Baker Creek Heirloom Seeds, Missouri, www.rareseeds.com

Dry-cured Smithfield or Virginia hams: The Genuine Smithfield Ham Shoppe, 224 Main Street, Smithfield, Virginia 23430; (757) 357-1798. Try www.smithfieldhams.com. Or drop by 421 Prince George St., Williamsburg, Virginia.

BIBLIOGRAPHY

Asquam Ancestral Cookery: Recipes, Remedies & Household Hints. Edited by Mary Elizabeth Piper Nielsen and Ann Marie Nielsen Maguire. (Holderness, New Hampshire. No date).

Correspondence (1838-1864), Letters Arranged by Place of Origin, New York-North Carolina, Alexandre Vattemare Papers, Manuscripts and Archives Division, New York Public Library.

Croly, Mrs. J. C. *Jennie June's American Cookery Book* (New York: The American News Company, 1866).

Country Cooking: A home cook book of one thousand selected recipes. (Kansas: Capper Publications, 1907).

John Grafton. *The American West in the Nineteenth Century.* (New York: Dover Publications, Inc., 1992).

Mrs. D. A. Lincoln. *Mrs. Lincoln's Boston Cook Book.* (Boston: Roberts Brothers, 1883).

Martha McCulloch-Williams. *Dishes & Beverages of the Old South.* Facsimile of the 1913 original, with a new introduction by John Egerton. (Knoxville: The University of Tennessee Press, 1988).

Mrs. McLintock's Receipts for Cookery and Pastry-Work. 1736. Introduction and Glossary by Iseabail Macleod. (Aberdeen: University Press, 1986).

"*Nineteenth-Century Farm Life,*" leaflet for The History Farm, Kings Mountain State Park, Blacksburg, S.C. No date.

Kay Morrow, Editor. *The New England Cook Book of Fine Old Yankee Recipes.* (Reading, Pa.: Culinary Arts Press, 1936).

BIBLIOGRAPHY

Mary Ronald. *The Century Cook Book*. (New York: Century Publishing, 1895).

Amelia Simmons. *American Cookery*, 1796. Updated and introduction by Iris Ihde Frey. (Greens Farm, CT: The Silverleaf Press, 1984).

Andrew Smith, Editor in Chief, *The Oxford Encyclopedia of Food and Drink in America* (New York: Oxford University Press, 2004).

Keith Stavely and Kathleen Fitzgerald. *America's Founding Food: The Story of New England Cooking*. (Chapel Hill: University of North Carolina Press, 2004).

The Fruit Book. (Chicago: Woman's World Magazine Co., Inc., 1928).

Barbara M. Walker. *The Little House Cookbook: Frontier Foods from Laura Ingalls Wilder's Classic Stories*. (New York: HarperTrophy, 1979).

William Woys Weaver, *America Eats: Forms of Edible Folk Art*. (New York: Harper & Row, 1989).

Cornpone, hog jaw and salt are fit for a king.
-- Kentucky proverb

RECIPE INDEX

RECIPE INDEX

RECIPE INDEX

RECIPE INDEX